COMMUNICATION PROBLEMS
IN MENTAL RETARDATION

OMMUNICATION PROBLEMS
N MENTAL RETARDATION:
diagnosis and management

HEROLD S. LILLYWHITE
University of Oregon Medical School

DORIS P. BRADLEY
University of North Carolina

HARPER & ROW, PUBLISHERS
New York, Evanston, and London

Communication Problems in Mental Retardation:
Diagnosis and Management

70072

Contents

v

Foreword

The realization that mental retardation is a major waste of the nation's resources and the growing body of scientific knowledge that could be used to reduce this waste have led the federal government to provide support for a variety of programs related to mental retardation.

Striking directly at some of the prenatal conditions that result in mental retardation, projects have been established to provide better health services to mothers and to their infants for the hazardous first year of life. Federal support also has made possible the rapid development of centers where children suspected of being mentally retarded can receive a comprehensive diagnosis and a sound plan of management. Grants to research centers have enabled these institutions to seek more intensively for information related to mental retardation—probing especially into the nature of those inborn errors of metabolism that devastate the central nervous system.

All these efforts to prevent mental retardation, to reduce and ameliorate its effects, and to provide appropriate management demand that training institutions produce additional specialists in many fields. One of these, certainly, is the field of speech pathology and audiology.

The speech pathologist and audiologist have long dealt with mental retardation, for one of its early signs is the child's inadequate or inappropriate speech and language patterns. The clinician's training, however, like that in many other disciplines, has often been in environments that did not include a multidisciplinary approach to mental retardation. Like others, the field of speech pathology and audiology has needed the opportunity offered by the new university-affiliated centers for the study of mental retardation.

With federal funds for buildings, for staff, and for traineeships, the concept of the university-affiliated center is one in which multiple disciplines work and train together. This concept of interrelated training requires that each profession clearly determines those contributions for which it is uniquely responsible. To do this requires that each discipline understand the responsibilities and limitations of other disciplines. Herold S. Lillywhite and Doris P. Bradley have aimed *Communication Problems in Mental Retardation: Diagnosis and Management* directly at this new way of serving the mentally retarded. This text lays the groundwork for the understanding of a multidisciplinary approach to training even for those whose training is not to be taken at such a university-affiliated center.

Mental retardation must be viewed in its broadest definition, and the efforts of speech pathologists and audiologists must be focused on total communicative behavior if effective diagnosis and management are to be offered. Specialists must be trained, at the outset, to function in multidisciplinary settings if services are to be comprehensive and intensive as well. This text develops such an approach. Hopefully, it will spur those who already have dedicated themselves to the mentally retarded and will encourage others to find rewards in serving those who learn slowly.

DONALD A. HARRINGTON, PH.D.
Speech and Hearing Consultant
Children's Bureau

Preface

The authors' purpose in writing this book is three-fold: (1) to prepare a relatively simple, short volume that can be used as a general and specific guide for those speech pathologists and audiologists, teachers of the mentally retarded, and others involved in the diagnosis and management of communication problems of mentally retarded children; (2) to outline briefly the total framework within which the diagnosis and management of the mentally retarded must be considered; (3) to attempt to combine some of the significant traditional concepts and approaches toward mental retardation with newer, broader concepts and probable future trends.

The book is not intended as a "how-to" book of the

recipe variety. The authors believe that the speech pathologists and audiologists involved with mentally retarded children already have sufficient clinical skill to be able to adapt to most speech therapy needs of the retarded. On the other hand, we have attempted to stress what frequently is a neglected aspect of the management of the retarded: that is, the necessity for training in the basic language and communication skills. We have, however, included a chapter on specific techniques that can be used to improve the speech of the retarded. We have chosen to base these techniques on the various processes of human communication rather than to follow the traditional patterns of classification according to etiological factors. We believe this kind of approach, both to diagnosis and management, is more appropriate for the retarded than the traditional one is.

With the belated realization that the mentally retarded child is a multiply handicapped child, a tremendous increase of activity involving various professional disciplines has occurred. For this reason, those specialists most concerned with improving communication skills of the retarded are in great demand. Their participation will be in cooperation with many different specialists working together for a common goal of improving the lot of the retarded, rather than having individual therapies being carried out in relative isolation. One aspect of the "new look," then, is the necessity for the communication specialists to be able to function as members of multidiscipline diagnostic and management teams.

The authors believe that no one can deal adequately in diagnosis or management of specific aspects of any handicapping condition without understanding a great deal about all related aspects of the handicap. This is especially true with mental retardation. Diagnosis and treatment of the communication problems of a retarded child will be much more fruitful when they are based on an understanding of the significant etiological factors that may underlie the retardation, and knowledge concerning the physical, mental, social, psychological, and educational components of the retardate and his environment. For these reasons, we have presented a somewhat sketchy, but we hope adequate, background of information in the early chapters of the book as a framework for the approaches to speech and language diagnosis and management that are presented in the final chapters. For the student, diagnostician, clinician, or other specialist, we believe this kind of framework will be valuable.

The authors wish to express appreciation to Drs. Nancy Marshall, Wilma Carson, John Gullickson, and Norton Young—all of whom are staff members of the University of Oregon Medical School Multi-Discipline Clinic for the Mentally Retarded—for providing materials, assistance, and guidance in the preparation of certain portions of this book. We are especially grateful to Dr. Marshall for reading the manuscript and offering many valuable suggestions, and to Dr. Carson for guidance as to the medically related sections of the book. To graduate students David Haugen and David Stensland we also offer our thanks for reading the manuscript and making careful and thoughtful observations.

HEROLD S. LILLYWHITE
DORIS P. BRADLEY

COMMUNICATION PROBLEMS
IN MENTAL RETARDATION

CHAPTER *1*

Background

Of all the types of human problems resulting in major communication disorders, mental retardation is perhaps least understood, most puzzling, and most neglected by speech and hearing specialists; yet communication disorders arising from various kinds of mental retardation far outnumber disorders resulting from any other single problem. The misunderstanding and neglect, however, can be explained as being somewhat typical of individuals in many other professions, both medical and nonmedical, and in society as a whole. Social recognition of the mentally subnormal apparently has existed for almost as long as man has existed as a social being. Acceptance, however, has been a very long time coming—and recognition of

1

the fact that the mentally retarded individual is a social being worthy of study and help is a very recent social achievement. Yet even today a shocking amount of superstition, misunderstanding, mistreatment, and neglect of the mentally retarded exists in many areas of the civilized world.

Attitudes

Within the last decade a striking change has been evidenced in attitudes toward social responsibility for the mentally retarded. The result has been the stimulation of a great amount of research, some very promising habilitation programs, and generally widespread acceptance by educators and the public of the responsibility for improving the lot of the mentally retarded insofar as it is possible. This forward movement has been greatly stimulated by activities of the federal government and, in particular, by President John F. Kennedy, who drew national attention to the problems of the retarded, and whose Committee for the Study of Mental Retardation (49) outlined many of the problems and made a number of far-reaching recommendations.

A great deal of confusion, however, still exists concerning the problem of retardation—exactly what is meant by the terms referring to mental retardation, the wide scope of problems resulting in subnormal mental functioning, and the most effective means of management of the retarded. For this reason it is important for speech pathologists and audiologists to be aware of the existing confusions and to be able to focus their point of view in as intelligent and constructive a manner as possible.

Definition

The task of defining retardation is not a simple one because, at least from the standpoint of the psychologist, mental subnormality does not in itself constitute a disease but rather an effect in the human organism that may result from any one of many diseases or from psychological or environmental conditions. The definition of mental retardation depends, at least in part, on the standards of society. Masland, Sarason, and Gladwin (66) state the problem this way:

In our society the problem looms large—statistically, financially and emotionally; in most European societies it is inconsequential, confined to cases of severe pathological defect who are cared for as long as they live, with a minimum of distress or dislocation. The difference lies in culturally determined attitudes, behaviors, and criteria of social acceptability. . . . Even the child with a severe defect must be viewed as deficient relative to cultural standards of acceptability; the cause of his deficiency may be organic, but its magnitude is dependent upon social criteria.

From these discussions, it seems clear that a "mentally subnormal" individual in one culture may not be considered subnormal in another culture. Even in this country there is considerable question, in spite of generalized standards of mental measurement, as to who is subnormal and who is not. This is especially true for individuals in adult life, who, at one time, appeared unable to learn according to standardized methods and rate, yet who take their places as constructive adult members of society and are able to function independently. Definitions of mental retardation, then, are at best somewhat transitory and provincial with respect to time and place.

A great many terms have been used to describe the condition of the individual who is functioning at a subnormal level, among which are "mental subnormality," "mental deficiency," "feeble-mindedness," "mentally handicapped," "amentia" (meaning, literally, "lack of mind"), "brain injured," "pseudoretardation" (meaning retarded intellectual function due to emotional or environmental factors), and some other terms not in current use.

In 1959 the American Association on Mental Deficiency (33) recommended the use of the term "mental retardation," which they feel "incorporates all of the meanings that have been ascribed historically to such concepts as amentia, feeble-mindedness, mental deficiency, mental subnormality, idiocy, imbecility, and moronity, etc." The Association has defined mental retardation as "all degrees of mental defect due to arrested or imperfect mental development as a result of which the person afflicted is incapable of competing on equal terms with his normal fellows, or of managing himself or his affairs with ordinary prudence." The Association further describes mental retardation as referring to "sub-average general intellectual functioning which originates during the developmental period, and is associated with impairment in one or more of the following: (1) Maturation; (2) Learning; (3) Social Adjustment."

Jordan (45) also uses the term mental retardation and says:

. . . in general terms, it describes inherent limitations of the individual's growth and ability to perform tasks of abstraction and organization, and it sets limits to the ceiling his abilities will eventually reach. Interests, skills and the like are usually those of a younger person, and the level of performance in tasks of an intellectual nature is below expectation.

As the term mental retardation appears to be most widely used, and the definition of the American Association on Mental Deficiency perhaps most widely accepted, such language will be used in this book. It will be noted that all of the definitions mentioned imply that the mentally retarded individual is deficient in his capacity to learn on an intellectual basis and in his capacity to adapt on a behavioral basis. Thus the concept of "measured intelligence" and "adaptive behavior" is utilized in these definitions. The original purpose of intelligence tests was to measure only the individual's ability to perform educational tasks according to standardized age levels and to predict an individual's ability to learn in a regular educational setting.

These tests also measure more or less accurately the individual's adaptive behavior, that is, his ability to respond to social and other stimuli. According to Spreen (85): "The studies of abstraction seem to indicate that a very close relationship exists between language and thought processes and that some kind of 'inner language' or verbal mediation may be essential to intelligent behavior." Relationships of verbal behavior to motor behavior and visual learning behavior are sampled in general intelligence testing. Such tests, however, are not infallible, as will be seen later, because of the many additional factors that enter into the matter of mental retardation.

Classification

Many methods of classification have been used for the mentally retarded. The American Association on Mental Deficiency classifies levels of retardation based on the measurement by the Stanford Binet and Wechsler Scales, as shown in Table 1.

T A B L E 1. CLASSIFICATION OF MENTAL RETARDATION

CLASSIFICATION	IQ RANGE	
Level	*Binet*	*Wechsler*
Profound retardation	Below 20	Below 25
Severe retardation	20– 35	25– 39
Moderate retardation	36– 51	40– 54
Mild retardation	52– 67	55– 69
Borderline intelligence	68– 83	70– 84
Average intelligence	84–116	85–115

SOURCE: R. Heber, "A Manual of Terminology and Classification in Mental Retardation," Monograph Supplement, Second Edition to *American Journal of Mental Deficiency*, Vol. 65, No. 1, 1960–61. Pp. 499–500.

A different kind of classification has been established in terms of the individual's educability. From this classification the terms "educable," "trainable," and "custodial" have come into widespread use in diagnosis of the mentally retarded. Table 2 shows the IQ and mental age ranges in the three classifications, and includes a description of the meanings of these three groupings.

The speech pathologists in clinical settings are likely to be primarily concerned with the educable group of persons who usually live at home. The trainable group receives a great deal of attention in institutional settings and in an increasing number of school situations. The institutionalized mentally retarded generally will be in the

T A B L E 2. CHARACTERISTICS OF MENTAL RETARDATION

IQ 0–25 (MA 0–2)	IQ 25–49 (MA 2–7)	IQ 50–75[a] (MA 7–10)
Very severe	Severe	Moderate
Custodial	Trainable	Educable (slow learning)
Dependent	Semidependent	Independent or marginally independent
Incapable of self-care	Can learn self-care and to adjust socially. Incapable of academic work. A few capable of very simple work in a protected work situation.	Can develop social and occupational adequacy; capable of unskilled or semi-skilled work. Can achieve academic work to third, fourth, or fifth grade level, sometimes sixth.

[a] IQ 75–89 is borderline, sometimes classified as mentally retarded, sometimes normal.

SOURCE: Christine P. Ingram, *Education of the Slow-Learning Child.* New York, The Ronald Press, Third Edition. Copyright © 1960, The Ronald Press Company, New York.

trainable and custodial classifications and many of them will be seen at least for diagnostic purposes in speech and hearing clinics. Audiologists will be concerned with hearing assessments of children at all three levels, when such is possible.

Incidence and prevalence

There are many ways to report the incidence and prevalence of mental retardation; none of them is entirely accurate because of the way the information is gathered and the instability of standards determining mental retardation. Information reported by the U. S. Public Health Service, Department of Health, Education, and Welfare, in January 1962 (49), and by the President's Committee on Mental Retardation in June 1967 (25), is perhaps as reliable as any data available up to this time. Some general conclusions reached from these data are as follows. Approximately five million persons in this country are retarded. Most of these persons are children. Mental retardation disables nineteen times as many people as diabetes, twenty times as many as tuberculosis, twenty-five times as many as muscular dystrophy, and six times as many as infantile paralysis. Every year 126,000 babies are born who will be mentally retarded. In 1967 approximately 201,000 of the retarded were confined to institutions, at a cost of more than $300,000,000 annually. The other 96 percent were living in private homes. Among these children, 587,722 were in school classes for the educable retarded and 89,252 were (in 1967) in classes for the trainable. The financial, social, and psychological cost of providing for them at home and in local community and school situations represents a staggering burden to each affected family and to the community.

The foregoing figures provided by the U. S. Public Health Service are in quite close agreement with estimates made by a number of authorities on mental retardation. There is variation, however, ranging from a low of five-and-one-half million retarded individuals to an estimate as high as ten million. The wide variety of estimates as to the total number of retarded people comes from different classifications of mental retardation and different methods of sampling. The most commonly accepted total is between five and six million individuals with measured intelligence quotients below 70. If the group usually called "slow learners," with IQs between 70 and 85, were included, the total number of retarded would be more than doubled, or more than ten million.

The Department of Health, Education, and Welfare estimates that there are approximately two million retarded children of school age. Ingram (40) has indicated that from 2 to 3 percent of school-age children fall into the IQ ranges below 75, and that there are 15 to 18 percent of the school children in the IQ range from 75 to 89. She implies that most of those children in the latter group, while having some mental limitations, can succeed reasonably well in a normal classroom, but that 2 percent of the school population have mental limitations so severe that their failure to succeed in school with average children is conspicuous.

Prevalence of speech, language, and hearing disorders

If there are 2 to 3 percent of school-age children with IQs below 75, and 15 to 18 percent in the IQ range 75 to 89, this means that a very sizeable population of children both in and out of school are in a very high-risk group from the standpoint of speech, language, and hearing disorders. Speech pathologists and audiologists in clinics, private practice, and school situations in the past have had to deal with a fairly large number of retarded children, and in the future can expect increasing pressure for offering both diagnostic and remedial assistance for large numbers of the mentally retarded. Much attention in the community and the schools is being focused very directly and strongly on the retarded, and there is increasing demand for help with their multiple handicaps. The handicaps of speech, language, and hearing certainly are central in many of these children, and they must be dealt with.

Data are not at all conclusive with respect to the extent and prevalence of speech, language, and hearing disorders in the mentally retarded, but a number of reports have made it possible to draw conclusions. Nearly all investigators have concluded that institutionalized retardates present more frequent and more severe speech, language, and hearing problems than do noninstitutionalized retardates. Data from several studies (79) (80) (41) indicate that roughly from 60 to 89 percent of institutionalized retardates have communication problems of a serious nature.

Also of interest to the speech pathologist and audiologist are the educable mentally retarded (IQ roughly 50 to 70), most of whom will be in schools or will be referred to clinics for help. Current data indicate that a considerably higher percentage of these children have communication problems than do other school children in the higher IQ ranges.

In a 1962–1963 survey of educable mentally retarded children in the Portland, Oregon, public schools (4) 12 percent were found to have speech and/or language disorders, compared with 4.5 percent in the same survey among the nonretarded. In an unpublished report from the Crippled Children's Division of the University of Oregon Medical School, Young (95) and Marshall (65) found a variety of problems in a study of 200 children, ranging in IQ from 40 to 70. These children were examined extensively over a 5-week period in the Crippled Children's Division's Mental Retardation Program. None of the children showed speech and language skills commensurate with chronological age. All of the children showed speech and language functioning in one way or another significantly inferior to expectations based upon mental age.

Thirty-nine percent showed delays in verbal expression and 43 percent had articulation problems. Eighteen percent showed disturbance in motor control for articulation. Voice quality disturbances were present in 21 percent in the form of excess nasality, huskiness, and other deviations. Excess nasality seemed to be a result of palatal deviations and sluggish use of palatopharyngeal structures for speech. Young (95) and Marshall (65) concluded:

1) Speech, language, and hearing problems have a far higher incidence above and beyond general lag in language

development than in the normal population. 2) The kind of speech and hearing problems retardates may possess are highly varied. Speech and language function does not necessarily correlate closely with mental age. A child of ten with a mental age of five may or may not be communicating as well as a five-year-old child. Many factors contribute to speech and language development in addition to learning ability.

Prevalence of hearing loss also is higher among all levels of the mentally retarded than among the nonretarded. Admittedly, hearing testing of the mentally retarded is complicated, but competent audiologists have been able to do reliable pure-tone testing on most retarded children with IQ 40 or above (84). For those subjects found difficult to test by the usual pure-tone methods, operant conditioning and other infant testing techniques have produced reasonably accurate results. As is true with speech and language deficiencies, the incidence of hearing loss increases with lowered mental functioning, with institutionalized retardates presenting much higher percentages of hearing loss.

Holmes and Peletier (37) surveyed the hearing of retardates at Pineland Hospital and Training Center and then compared their findings with other surveys available. The hearing loss criterion was an average threshold of 15 dB (ASA) or poorer for the three speech frequencies, 500, 1000, and 2000 Hz in either ear. Of the 824 retardates who were cooperative for the test procedures, 139 (16.8 percent) had impaired hearing in the speech frequencies. An additional 3.3 percent had losses in frequencies above 4000 Hz. This is in very close agreement with the study of Lloyd and Reid (60), who reported that 76 of 482 retardates (16 percent) tested at the Parsons

Training Center had impaired hearing according to the same criterion used in the Pineland population. These two major studies further support the impression that hearing loss is greater among the retarded than among the nonretarded.

Four investigators, Kodman (52), Matthews (67), and Schlanger and Gottsleben (80), have summarized a large number of studies and investigations of hearing loss among institutionalized retardates and report that the prevalence ranges from 18 to 50 percent. The Schlanger and Gottsleben figures are quite representative of the others. They found approximately 55 percent had normal hearing, 14 percent had only slight deviations at extreme frequencies, 28 percent had moderate losses, 6 percent were hard-of-hearing, and 1 percent, deaf. Seventeen percent of the population were "nontestable."

In the reports by Young (95) and Marshall (65) mentioned previously, 12 percent demonstrated conductive hearing losses of 20 to 40 dB by pure-tone and speech-reception testing. In nearly all cases hearing loss had not been suspected by the parents. Five percent had sensori-neural hearing impairment. The remainder had hearing loss generally caused by middle ear disease.

Not only do institutionalized retardates have a high prevalence of hearing loss, but it also is true that the educable mentally retarded in school populations have from two to three times more hearing loss than the non-retarded population. In an unpublished report (2) of hearing testing of the school population in the state of Oregon in 1963–1964, 2235 children in special achievement classes (educable mentally retarded) were tested.

Seventeen percent of these children were found to have a referable hearing loss—that is, a loss of 20 dB or more in the frequencies 500, 1000, and 2000 in either ear, or an average loss of 25 dB or more in the higher frequencies (3000, 4000, and 6000 in either ear). This loss is approximately five times the prevalence of 3.3 percent found in the over-all normal school population in Oregon for the same year.

Approximately two-thirds of the children with hearing loss were found to have conductive loss. The remainder had sensorineural or mixed loss. The report points out that this prevalence figure for the educable retarded in Oregon is in sharp contrast to the approximately 4 to 5 percent among the nation's normal school-age children who exhibit a hearing loss.

It may be concluded, then, that among the retarded—both institutionalized and school populations—approximately four to five times more hearing loss is found than among the nonretarded school population, with the institutionalized retardates showing considerably more loss.

The exact reasons for the greater prevalence of hearing loss among the retarded are not known. It has been speculated that the retarded may exhibit more conductive loss due to middle ear infection because of lack of nasal and upper respiratory cleanliness. Another possibility is that, as the retarded child appears to be more subject to upper respiratory infection, he would have more middle ear problems. A structural difference in the ear of mongoloids, found by Young (95) and Marshall (65) in studies previously quoted, results in a smaller external auditory canal. These investigators found a great number of impacted ears among the mongoloids, and attributed hearing loss to this factor in several cases. At the moment, however, no definitive studies of the causes of the greater prevalence of hearing loss among retardates are known to give positive information that would account for this phenomenon.

The foregoing information suggests that the speech pathologist and the audiologist are likely to be presented with communication problems of the mentally retarded in almost any situation in which they work. In schools the fairly sizeable number of speech and hearing defective children in the educable retarded group will be of concern to the speech clinician. In clinics and private practice, those retarded children with more severe communication deficiencies will be referred for diagnosis and management to the speech pathologist and audiologist by physicians, agencies, and parents. As the numbers of retardates with communication problems are considerable, and as there is increasing attention being directed toward the mentally retarded, a knowledge of the problems and procedures involved becomes increasingly important to the speech pathologist and audiologist.

Supplemental references

Begab, M. J. "The Mentally Retarded Child: A Guide to Services and Social Agencies." *Children's Bureau Publication* No. 409, U. S. Government Printing Office, Washington, D.C., 1963. Pp. 1–2.

Brown, S. F. "A Note on Speech Retardation in Mental Deficiency." *Pediatrics,* Vol. 16, No. 2, 1955. Pp. 272–273.

Covert, Cathy. *Mental Retardation: A Handbook for the Primary Physician*. Report of the American Medical Association Conference on Mental Retardation, Chicago, April, 1964. Reprinted from the *Journal of the American Medical Association*, Vol. 191, No. 3, 1965. Pp. 1–141.

Gardner, W. I., and H. W. Nisonger. "A Manual on Program Development in Mental Retardation; Guidelines for Planning, Development, and Coordination of Programs for the Mentally Retarded at State and Local Levels." *American Journal of Mental Deficiency*, Vol. 66, No. 4, 1962.

Harrison, S. "A Review of Research in Speech and Language Development of the Mentally Retarded." *American Journal of Mental Deficiency*, Vol. 63, No. 1, 1958. Pp. 236–240.

CHAPTER *2*

*E*tiological factors
and general characteristics

A great deal is known about the conditions that result in mental retardation, but many aspects of specific causes and the resultant types of mental deficiency are not clearly defined. Insofar as possible, it is useful to determine specific original etiological factors because many of them can be manipulated for better management of the retarded, and a few can be controlled and even eliminated.

Etiological factors

More than one hundred different conditions resulting in mental retardation have been recognized and described

17

in the literature. The majority of these conditions are rare, and the resultant numbers of retardates are perhaps not significant. Yannet (94) has indicated that about 20 percent of the etiological conditions known occur with sufficient frequency to have practical importance with respect to mental retardation. In a large population of institutionalized mentally retarded, Yannet found only 10 percent of the causes to be related to conditions occurring during birth or thereafter. The remaining 90 percent were related to prenatally determined etiological conditions. At least one-half of this 90 percent, he concluded, were genetically determined.

There is little need in this discussion to consider in detail the many causes of mental retardation. Table 3 is a simplified classification of mental retardation according to etiological factors, adapted from the medical classification of the American Association on Mental Deficiency (42).

Table 3 includes most of the important conditions that might result in mental retardation. Many of them need not be discussed at this point; some, however, deserve mention. The question of heredity in mental retardation always has been an important one, and looms large in the minds of parents of a retarded child as well as those associated with them. As was seen in Yannet's study (94), perhaps half of the prenatally determined cases of mental retardation were found to be genetically determined. Most lay persons and many professionals have associated genetic incidence of this sort with hereditary factors. It must be remembered that genetic transmission is simply a mechanism by which a condition can be passed on from parent to child. In itself it is not a cause. It will

T A B L E 3. SIMPLIFIED MEDICAL CLASSIFICATION OF
MENTAL RETARDATION

Category 1—MR associated with cerebral infections, both prenatal and postnatal.

Category 2—MR associated with intoxications such as: toxemia of pregnancy, other maternal intoxication, bilirubin, and postimmunization intoxication.

Category 3—MR associated with conditions due to trauma or physical agents such as: prenatal injury, mechanical injury at birth, aspyhxia at birth, or postnatal injury.

Category 4—MR associated with diseases or conditions due to disorders of metabolism, growth, or nutrition. Some of these are cerebral lipoidosis, phenylketonuria, histidinema galactosemia, disorders of protein metabolism, and disorders of carbohydrate metabolism, arachnodactyly, hypothroidism, and gargoylism.

Category 5—MR associated with diseases and conditions due to new growths, including neurofibromatosis, trigeminal angiomatosis, tubersclerosis, and intracranial neoplasms.

Category 6—MR associated with diseases and conditions due to prenatal influence resulting in congential cerebral defects, cranial anomalies, Laurence-Biedl syndrome, and mongolism.

Category 7—MR associated with conditions due to uncertain cause, with the structural reaction manifest in conditions of brain sclerosis and cercbellar degeneration.

Category 8—MR due to uncertain cause, with the functional reaction alone manifest in the following: cultural-familial MR, psychogenic MR associated with environmental deprivation, psychogenic MR associated with emotional disturbances, and MR associated with psychotic disorders.

SOURCE: G. A. Jervis. "Medical Aspects of Mental Retardation." *Journal of Rehabilitation*. Vol. 28, No. 6, 1962. Pp. 34–36.

be seen in Table 3 that a number of categories—4, 5, 6, 7 —include conditions that can be genetically transmitted.

The usual concept of heredity is that a child of low mentality is a result of a familial condition—ancestors of low mentality. While this sometimes is the case, more frequently deficiencies resulting in low mentality may be genetically transmitted to a child from perfectly normal ancestors in the form of a specific disorder. Such appears to be the case with a number of the metabolic disorders, cranial anomalies, growth and nutrition disturbances, and mongolism, among others. It becomes important, then, to keep in mind that the usual concept of heredity and mental retardation probably has little validity.

Category 8 of Table 3 deserves some attention. Mental retardation occurring as a result of any of these "functional" factors frequently has been termed "pseudo-retardation." What is important here is that such conditions as subcultural familial environments, environmental deprivation, and emotional disturbances (including psychotic disorders) can result in mental retardation as severe and permanent as that resulting from organic causes. It has been recognized that a child can be both mentally retarded and psychotic, schizophrenic, or autistic, or can be mentally retarded and also happen to be in a cultural or environmental situation that is substandard; but the concept of these factors as causes of mental retardation is not widespread. This concept deserves careful attention from the individual working with the mentally retarded.

The question of "brain damage" assumes major importance in relation to mental retardation. An examination of the many causes and mechanisms resulting in mental retardation indicates that most of these conditions eventually result in some form of damage to the brain. Actually mental retardation itself suggests "brain deficiency," which generally is thought not to be reversible. In this sense, then, nearly all forms of mental retardation may be thought of as resulting from "brain damage."

The concept of "specific brain damage" and "generalized brain damage" has come into quite general use. This concept suggests that damage to the brain over a widespread area of the cortex results in mental retardation or generalized retarded mental functioning while more limited damage to the brain in specific areas results in reduced brain function in these areas alone—leaving other areas of the brain undamaged and capable of functioning normally. This latter condition has been considered by many professionals not to be "true mental retardation," but has been described variously as "neurological dysfunction," "specific brain damage," or just "brain damage" that results in inconsistent deficiencies—frequently those in the speech and language areas. In other cases the specific damage to the brain has resulted in crippling conditions such as are found in cerebral palsy.

It is significant that these specific disorders due to damage to the brain may be somewhat separate from, but accompanying, generalized mental retardation; or, as implied in the above classification, may result in generalized mental retardation. It is of utmost importance that etiological factors be determined insofar as is possible so that the types of cerebral dysfunction might be defined and the resultant communication disorder thereby better understood and treated.

General characteristics

It is as unwise to generalize about the mentally retarded as it is about any other group of individuals; however, within the various classification groups in mental retardation, there are some specific intellectual and behavioral characteristics that can apply to the majority of retardates to a greater or lesser degree—according to the amount of retardation, as well as physical, environmental, and educational factors. Jordan (45) concludes his chapter on "Characteristics of the Mentally Retarded" as follows:

This much seems clear; the retarded present a picture of dysfunction in which many aspects of behavior are involved at least to some extent. The retarded person has a limited grasp of abstractions. He does not have the capacity to foresee all the consequences of his actions. He has potential for a limited group of occupations. He is not inherently dangerous, but his presence may be disturbing to others. He has the capacity to profit from our attempts to help him.

Levenson and Bigler (56) list a number of mental, behavioral, and medical conditions characteristic of many of the mentally retarded. These include: lowered intelligence; lack of concentration; delayed neuromuscular development; hyper- or hypoactivity; speech, hearing, vision, and emotional problems; convulsions; paralysis; temperature, and pulse aberrations; respiration irregularities; susceptibility of the respiratory system to infection; gastrointestinal tract difficulties; circulatory system problems; genitourinary tract problems; skin ailments; and miscellaneous conditions such as grinding the teeth, drooling, slowness in gaining weight, and stocky body build with below-normal height.

Educators have listed many characteristics that bear on the individual's inability to learn. This list includes such aspects as slow reaction time, limited range of interests, inadequate adaptive and associative abilities, limited ability to work with abstractions and to generalize, limited ability to evaluate material for relevancy, inadequate powers of self-correction, inadequate motivation and erratic drives, short attention span, short memory span, lack of originality and creative ability, inability to analyze and give critical judgment, inability to set up work standards, and inability to project adequately beyond the local situation.

It should be noted that this list of characteristics is so extensive that it covers almost all the physical, behavioral, and educational aspects of any individual. Most investigators are in substantial agreement that most of these conditions may be characteristic of many retardates, but it is obvious that there are wide variations among the retarded as well as the nonretarded. It is safe to conclude, however, that the mentally retarded individual is generally not only retarded in brain function but is also retarded as a whole —the degree depending on the extent of the initial damage and usually correlating with the measured intellectual and behavioral capacities. That is, the higher the IQ and the more nearly the mental age approaches the chronological age, the less generalized retardation and the fewer other deficiencies will be found.

The foregoing discussion of etiological factors and characteristics in mental retardation should suggest several responsibilities to the speech pathologist and audiologist charged with participation in diagnosis and treatment of the retarded child or adult. In the first place, there is need for recognition of the wide variety of etiological factors possible. An understanding of the nature of the damage that may be caused by any of these factors, as suggested by the extensive list of characteristics, will make diagnosis and management much more meaningful. Such understanding also will make it evident that diagnosis and management of retardates cannot be done by any one specialist, regardless of his specialty or competence.

Ideally the speech pathologist and the audiologist will be members of a diagnostic and management team, and as such they must be able to function with that team effectively—sometimes playing a leading role and sometimes a supporting role. When such a team is not available and the speech pathologist and audiologist find themselves working in relative isolation with the retarded, they must know where and how to secure the assistance of other specialists as it may be needed. (A more detailed discussion of who these specialists may be, and what roles they may play, will be found in a later chapter.)

Speech and language characteristics

Before discussing the specific characteristics of the speech and language of the retarded, it is necessary to make a distinction between speech and language and to define these two terms as they are used in this book.

Throughout the previous discussion, speech and language have been used together and sometimes synonymously. The authors prefer to think of all forms of verbal communication as "language." However, many investigators, clinicians, and writers dealing with communication and with communication disorders prefer to make a distinction between speech and language. Such a separation has considerable usefulness with respect to the treatment of communication disorders. Fairly typical of the distinctions made is that of Leberfeld (54):

Language can be defined as the ability to communicate ideas and feelings through the use of word symbols and the ability to understand and respond adaptively to the ideas and feelings of others as conveyed through the use of word symbols, while speech may be defined as the utterance of articulate sounds. Language is the higher function of the two, and unless language is present there can be no speech.

A somewhat different distinction has been made by the Committee on Language Development and Disorders of the American Speech and Hearing Association (64). They offer these definitions: "Language refers to the meaningful use of vocabulary and sentence structure, both oral and written. Speech refers to the process of producing the sounds, stress, rhythm, and intonation by which oral language is expressed."

Language also has been defined in terms of an organized structure embodying the receptive and expressive conceptual aspects of meaning, while speech is thought of as the mechanical means of articulating these symbolic concepts. Whatever the particular kind of distinction one wishes to make, the essential aspects for the speech clinician are that, as a social being, an individual needs to have some framework within which to receive, organize, and relate incoming verbal symbols in terms of meaning and to be able to organize and transmit an appropriate response through the use of verbal symbols. Language, then, may be thought of as the process of receiving, organizing, and symbolizing, and speech may be thought of as the process of transmitting by means of appropriately organized symbol units.

For any child to acquire the skills necessary for adequate communication, both verbal and nonverbal, he must develop certain physical, mental and psychosocial aspects.

PHYSICAL ASPECTS

Almost from the time the child is born he is influenced by sounds around him. Within the first few months of life he acquires skill in gross discrimination among sounds he hears. As he matures this sound discrimination becomes more highly differentiated, and his response matures in proportion to his ability to differentiate sound stimuli. By the age of 6 months his babbling and vocal play appear to reflect some manner of discrimination. Between 6 and 9 months considerable refinement of discrimination among sounds occurs. He not only responds to different voice qualities, different pitch levels, volume changes, and voiced and unvoiced sounds, but his ability to imitate many of these sounds also increases. By 9 months the child normally shows considerable variety in his own vocalizing, often following inflection and pitch patterns of the human voice.

In order for this development to take place, the child must have a relatively intact auditory mechanism. His hearing acuity must be adequate but, in addition to his acuity, the neural connections necessary for development of discrimination among speech sounds must be present.

The deaf child, for example, lacks the requisite of auditory acuity. A number of other children who have adequate auditory acuity lack discrimination facility. There is inadequate evidence as to the exact nature of this deficiency, but it is known that some individuals discriminate very poorly and in a delayed manner. This is true especially of retardates.

In addition to the requisite of hearing and discriminating speech sounds, the child also must have a relatively intact vocal mechanism in order to reproduce sounds and sound combinations that he has heard and discriminated. This means that the fine coordinations necessary for the reproduction of sounds need to mature within a normal age range, and must be free from defective neuromuscular and structural conditions. In other words, the child's motor functions must be adequate for the production of speech sounds.

How does the retarded child measure up with respect to the specific requisites mentioned? As has been noted earlier, he almost certainly will be delayed in the maturation of his neurophysiological processes. This means that, although his hearing acuity may be adequate, his discriminative ability is very likely to be delayed and perhaps deficient for the greater part of his life. Certainly the slower development of discriminative abilities throughout the period of language development influences language acquisition. In addition to this, the retarded child's ability to make the fine coordinations necessary to produce speech also is retarded and frequently quite defective. Very often these factors severely limit the child's experience through avenues of communication, with resultant social and psychological deprivation.

MENTAL ASPECTS

In order for the child to utilize in a systematic manner the sounds that he hears and discriminates, the associative and symbolic centers of the brain must be adequate to assign meaning to sounds, to relate these sounds to past experience, to abstract and organize into meaningful relationships, and, finally, to permit expression of his responses through some kind of symbol system. With these requisites the child is able to build vocabulary, that is, to relate meaning to stimuli, assign symbols to ideas (the process of abstracting), to relate parts to the whole of an idea, and to see the multiple aspects of a single idea. It is this ability to handle parts-whole relationships that enables the child to develop connected speech at such time as there is physiological readiness to reproduce it, and eventually to develop phrases, sentences, and larger structural units of thought.

In addition to these basic requisites, the child needs sufficient mental ability to develop inquisitiveness such as will lead him into exploration and the seeking of new experiences from which he can adapt and create new concepts that he can relate to previous experiences and concepts. Finally, he needs the ability to make use of these experiences, to expand them, to relate, and to generalize in a meaningful manner.

Not all mentally retarded children will be seriously lacking in these requisites, but it is safe to say that many of those in the educable, and still more of those in the trainable, group will be markedly deficient. Those in the custodial group almost universally will be either nonverbal or severely deficient. Even the "slow learning" group, that is, those with IQ between 70 and 89, have considerably more communication problems than those with IQ above 90. In the higher-level retardates, the educable and slow learners, one frequently expects late maturation of auditory discrimination and coordination of the motor skills of speech. The speech and language, however, while it may be somewhat inadequate, does not necessarily relate always to the IQ. Depth and richness of concepts and high-level abstraction, however, do relate to intelligence, so that one may expect, even in those retardates who display fairly adequate communicative abilities, a generally concrete and somewhat shallow conceptual pattern of language development and language usage.

These aspects, of course, relate to the lack of mental requisites for adequate language development. If the child lacks the basic ability to organize, integrate, and attach meaning to incoming verbal stimuli, certainly his verbal output will also be deficient. If he lacks the ability to see part-whole relationships and to proceed from the concrete to the abstract, he will have great difficulty in developing adequate connected speech and grammatical language structure.

PSYCHOSOCIAL ASPECTS

Given the necessary physical and mental attributes, the child still must have some fulfillment of certain basic psychological needs if he is to develop adequate communication. The emotionally deprived child frequently is a functionally retarded child. There is adequate clinical and experimental evidence that this same child also frequently is deficient in speech and language development. This apparently occurs because the need to be loved, wanted, and played with has not been fulfilled.

While still very young, the child needs to have someone to listen and respond to him, preferably with verbal response in the way of feedback to his own preverbal vocalization. Later the child needs to be helped to develop certain social skills adequate to allow for acceptance by his peers and by adults, and for the development of self-respect and a growing sense of confidence in his own abilities and in his relationships with others. This normal process of maturation, which leads to acceptance and adequate social relationships, is largely dependent upon adequate communication skills and, in return, enables the individual to interact effectively with his environment. Without the reasonably satisfactory fulfillment of the child's psychosocial needs, communication either does not develop or is seriously disrupted and deficient. This sets in motion a process whereby decreased efficiency in communication leads to increased social displacement and emotional disturbance that, in turn, lead to further decrease in communication adequacy.

In the psychosocial area, the retarded child also lacks the necessary requisites for the development of adequate communication. Gershenson and Schreiber (26) have summed up this deficiency in this manner:

The retarded child is often caught in a vicious spiral that is negative and limiting to his social development. The lack of social experiences leads to social retardation and ineptness in chronologically appropriate social skills, accompanied by emotional difficulties arising from feelings of rejection and deprivation; and the lack of social skills further limits the opportunities the retardate has of participating in social experiences.

Mentally retarded children must be taught many things which normal children learn spontaneously or incidentally. Often they must be taught to play and to help in developing creative qualities that give them fun and pleasure. When this has been achieved the retardate can gain the same satisfaction from participating in social activities as other people. These satisfactions derive from: a) Being recognized and accepted in the group situation; b) A sense of accomplishment in activities in which he is successfully interacting with his peers; c) The experience of self-expression, especially when making positive contributions to the group's activities; d) The enhancement of self-esteem; e) The feeling of "belonging."

From the very beginning, however, the retarded child is deprived of the opportunity to develop social skills in a normal manner and rarely is he in a situation in which he is given the special help he will need to learn these skills. As his early development is delayed, his parents frequently have found him not easy to love and accept, and because his verbalizing also is nonexistent or inappropriate and delayed, he has not been listened to or responded to, and there has been little or no feedback to stimulate the development of speech and language.

In addition to this situation, and sometimes because of it, the child's experience likely has been seriously limited. His lack of inquisitiveness, limited exploration and creativity, his inability to adapt, and the eventual lack of motivation for new experiences and his inability to relate new experiences to old ones have circumscribed his total learning opportunities. Clinically one frequently gets the very firm impression that the retarded child's inability to build adequate vocabulary and language structure may be as much a function of the limitations his retardation places upon him socially and experientially as the basic mental inadequacy. In any event, it is obvious that the retarded child will be limited in his speech and language development and the communication skills that he eventually will need.

Summary

In summary, we see that the general characteristics of retardates point to many areas and kinds of possible deficiencies. The influence of these deficiencies on the development of communication skills is considerable. The retarded child fails to meet most of the requisites necessary for speech and language learning because he is deficient in the necessary physical, mental, and psychosocial attributes. Fortunately, many of these deficiencies can be prevented or compensated for if adequate and early help is available. A key person in providing this help is the speech and hearing diagnostician and clinician. For that reason, the communication specialist must be entirely familiar with the specific deficiencies and potentialities of the retarded.

Supplemental references

Bateman, Barbara, and Janis Wetherell. "Psycholinguistic Aspects of Mental Retardation." *Mental Retardation,* Vol. 3, 1965. Pp. 8–13.

Begab, M. J. "The Mentally Retarded Child: A Guide to Services and Social Agencies." *Children's Bureau Publication* No. 404, U. S. Government Printing Office, Washington, D.C., 1963. Pp. 13–34.

Cortazzo, A. D. "Increasing Sociabilty for the Retarded Through Activity Programs." *Journal of Rehabilitation*, Vol. 30, No. 2, 1964. Pp. 13–15.

Howe, Clifford E. "A Comparison of Motor Skills of Mentally Retarded and Normal Children." *Exceptional Children*, Vol. 25, No. 8, 1959.

Jervis, G. A. "Factors in Mental Retardation." *Children*, Vol. 1, No. 6, 1954. Pp. 207–211.

Karlin, I. W., and Millicent Strazzula. "Speech and Language Problems of Mentally Deficient Children." *Journal of Speech and Hearing Disorders*, Vol. 17, No. 3, 1952. Pp. 286–294.

Kishimoto, K. "A Supplementary Study on the Etiology of Mental Retardation." *Japanese Journal of Child Psychiatry*, Vol. 4, 1963.

Koch, Richard, Nancy Ragsdale, Betty Graliker, Sylvia Schild, and Karol Fishler. "A Longitudinal Study of 143 Mentally Retarded Children (1955–1961)." *The Training School Bulletin*, Vol. 60, No. 1, 1963. Pp. 4–12.

Kugel, R. B., and J. Mohr. "Mental Retardation and Physical Growth." *American Journal of Mental Deficiency*, Vol. 68, No. 1, 1963. Pp. 41–48.

Richards, B. W. "Recent Advances in Medical Knowledge of Causes of Mental Retardation." *Canadian Medical Association Journal*, Vol. 89, 1963. Pp. 1230–1233.

Schlanger, B. B., and Gloria I. Galanowsky. "Auditory Discrimination Tasks Performed by Mentally Retarded and Normal Children." *Journal of Speech and Hearing Disorders*, Vol. 9, No. 3, 1966.

Stein, J. J. "Motor Function and Physical Fitness of the Mentally Retarded: A Critical Review." *Rehabilitation Literature*, Vol. 24, 1963. Pp. 230–242.

Wood, Nancy E. *Communication Problems and Their Effect on the Learning Potential of the Mentally Retarded Child*. U. S. Office of Education, C. R. P. #184, 1960.

CHAPTER *3*

Diagnosis of
mental retardation

The process of diagnosing mental retardation has unfortunately been subjected to enormous abuse, misunderstanding, and neglect. Since the development of intelligence tests there has been a widespread misconception among many professionals, and almost universally among laymen, that an IQ score constitutes a diagnosis of mental retardation or lack of it. With the development of diagnostic clinics and the accumulation of considerable research data concerning retardation, professional people have come to realize that it takes more than one person and an intelligence test to make a meaningful diagnosis of retardation in a child. The increasing use of the diagnostic team for many kinds of problems has demonstrated the necessity for use of this kind of procedure with the mentally retarded.

Differential diagnosis

The abnormal conditions accompanying mental retardation, as well as those that may be mistaken for mental retardation are numerous. A number of these, however, need specific comment because they need to be differentially evaluated in the diagnostic procedure. As these factors are discussed, the need for various specialists will be made clear. The part of the speech and hearing specialist as a member of the diagnostic team will be further amplified in later chapters, but his role will become quite obvious at this present point.

SLOW MOTOR DEVELOPMENT

Almost all clinical experience with the mentally retarded and research data reveal the fact that motor development in the retarded does not follow a normal pattern, but generally is delayed in proportion to the amount of retardation. Levenson and Bigler (56) indicate that about the only way anyone can evaluate mental functioning up to the age of 3 years is by comparing the child's activities with normal developmental landmarks in children. They have constructed a chart of normal development that goes through 24 months. This chart is by no means complete, but could be of use to any professional person or parent as a handy reference. Naturally, each professional will have other scales of development that give more detail than that information offered in Table 4.

TABLE 4.   EXPECTED NORMAL DEVELOPMENTAL PATTERN

Age (in months)	Characteristics
1	Hands fisted; hunger response; startle with loud sounds; smiles; chin up, regards surroundings.
2	Vocalizes by cooing back to mother; holds head up fairly well when pulled up by hands.
3	Has good head control; turns head from side to side.
4	Hands engage to grasp objects; eyes follow moving light.
5	Turns over; puts objects in mouth.
6	Sits fairly well; transfers objects from hand to hand.
7	Crawls; aware of strangers.
8	Stands with help and pushes down.
9	Index finger approach; beginning index-finger and thumb grasp.
10	Stands with support; holds own bottle; pat-a-cake, bye-bye, peek-a-boo.
11	Walks holding on; begins to obey "no-no."
12	Stands alone and may walk a few steps; repeats words, says single words.
18	Begins to obey simple commands; hurls ball; builds with 3–4 blocks; uses 10 or more words; toilet habits in daytime; names familiar objects.
24	Kicks ball; uses 6–7 blocks; makes 3-word sentences; walks up stairs.

SOURCE: A. Levenson and J. A. Bigler. *Mental Retardation in Infants and Children.* Copyright © 1960, Year Book Medical Publishers. Used by permission of Year Book Medical Publishers.

Kirk, Karnes, and Kirk (51) give a fairly complete and easily used developmental scale that begins at 3 months and goes to 7 years. It originally was prepared as a manual for parents of retarded children, but has been found very useful by many professional people as well. The authors demonstrate by example how a parent can make a gross evaluation of the developmental level of a child. They also have constructed a scale by which one might estimate possible attainments of the child after establishing the level of development. These levels of attainment are in terms of estimating whether the child will be educable, trainable, or totally dependent. The material is reproduced as Table 5.

Admittedly, the information in Table 5 gives a gross

T A B L E 5.   TABLE FOR ESTIMATING LEVEL OF RETARDATION

Level of development (years)	*Educable* if the child's age is (years)	*Trainable* if the child's age is (years)	*Totally dependent* if the child's age is (years)
1	1½–2	2–4	4 and above
1½	2–3	3 6	6 and above
2	2½–4	4–8	8 and above
2–3 (2½)	3½–5	5–10	10 and above
3	4–6	6–12	12 and above
3–4 (3½)	5–7	7–14	14 and above
4	5½–8	8–16	16 and above
4–5 (4½)	6–9	9 and above	—
5	7–10	10 and above	—
5–6 (5½)	7½–11	11 and above	—
6	8½–12	12 and above	—

SOURCE: Samuel A. Kirk, Merle B. Karnes, and Winifred D. Kirk. *You and Your Retarded Child.* New York, The Macmillan Co., 1956. P. 184.

evaluation and may be somewhat subject to misuse; but in the hands of parents, with the advice of a professional person, it probably permits avoidance of a great many errors that would occur without its use. It must be admitted that parents constantly are making comparisons and making their own evaluations, regardless of assistance from books or professional persons. Certainly they can do less harm with this kind of a guide than without it. In any event, it would be well for all professionals to be acquainted with these two excellent sources of developmental information because many parents are aware of them.

The significance of slow motor development from the standpoint of differential diagnosis is that, while these areas of retardation are fairly typical in the retarded child, they also are to be found in children with several other kinds of deviations—such as specific brain damage, cerebral palsy, and congenital or acquired neurophysiological deficiencies. Such children may or may not be mentally retarded; thus these factors of physical and developmental retardation, while of diagnostic significance in the mentally retarded, need to be clearly differentiated with respect to the other factors presented.

SPECIFIC BRAIN DAMAGE

The term specific brain damage has been used primarily in attempts to describe brain injury that results in neurological dysfunction and inconsistent retardation of specific areas of mental activity. Perhaps the most frequently encountered type of specific brain damage is that acquired either prenatally or postnatally, resulting in behavioral and symbolic disorders without motor problems.

The behavior of this kind of individual frequently has been referred to as the "Strauss syndrome," and often is characterized by hyperactivity, lack of attention, lack of inhibition, "catastrophic" reactions, lack of judgment, and difficulty in handling abstract concepts. Specific symbolic deficiencies in the form of any or several of the aphasias, dyslexia, agraphia, acalculia, and amusia may appear in almost any combination or singly.

It is important, then, to recognize that specific brain damage may result in or may accompany generalized mental retardation. Almost certainly it will result in some of the specific retarded functions mentioned, and particularly in cases of severe aphasia, there is great difficulty in distinguishing it from a more generalized mental retardation or from deafness.

CHILDHOOD SCHIZOPHRENIA

It originally was thought that childhood schizophrenia was a condition that followed after a period of normal development; for this reason it was not expected that such a condition would be confused with mental retardation. It now appears, however, that careful diagnostic procedures, including the taking of a detailed history, will reveal evidence of typical schizophrenic behavior from birth. This behavior includes disturbance of motility (i.e., bizarre patterns of movement), pronounced and prolonged withdrawal of interest from the external world, and disturbance in speech as the child becomes old enough to use speech. Michal-Smith (69) describes it in this manner:

The schizophrenic child, while he may appear mentally retarded and may score in the retarded range of intellectual testings often has a pattern of intellectual performance which is strikingly irregular and, in certain areas, superior.

Further evidence that schizophrenia may show a distinct developmental pattern from birth appears in the recent report by the World Health Organization (44), which states that there is a strong genetic component involved and that environment may be of relatively minor importance as a cause of schizophrenia. Huxley *et al.* (39) suggest that the disorder is an autosomal condition that, when heterozygous, has a selective advantage: resistance to stress.

INFANTILE AUTISM

Early infantile autism was described by Kanner (46) a number of years ago. It is easily mistaken for mental retardation by the hurried or unskilled diagnostician. Most sources agree that this condition can be manifested as early as in the first year of life by extreme withdrawal and a desire for the preservation of sameness. When seen in clinics, many of these children are completely withdrawn, resist human contact, and do not respond to voice or other human advances. Almost always they will perform extremely poorly on an intelligence test. However, adequate evaluation of many areas by a competent group may show that the child has average or superior ability in one or more areas of functioning.

OTHER EMOTIONAL DISTURBANCES

There are other emotional disturbances that can be mistaken for retardation. Among these are severe emotional trauma from a variety of causes, such as an extremely fearful situation, long periods of hospitalization, severe or brutal treatment at the hands of parents or others, or prolonged emotional deprivation. Any of these conditions can cause withdrawal and refusal of the organism to function in a normal manner intellectually or emotionally and sometimes physically. Prolonged emotional deprivation, in particular, is likely to produce a functional retardation that is extremely difficult to diagnose. If such deprivation has occurred, especially in the first 4 or 5 years of life, the consequences may be extremely severe and actual learning capacity may be permanently deficient.

HEARING

For generations countless hard-of-hearing and deaf children have been mistakenly labeled as mentally retarded, and in some cases institutionalized for a lifetime, when actually they had adequate learning potential. Most speech and hearing clinics can produce numerous records of hard-of-hearing children who have been labeled mentally retarded and frequently treated as such over long periods of time. Careful diagnostic procedures would have prevented this because it is possible, in most cases, for a competent audiologist to distinguish the deaf nonretarded child from the deaf retarded child. (Hearing evaluation will be discussed in detail in a later chapter.)

VISION

The child with a marked visual defect of congenital or early origin very frequently gives the appearance of mental retardation because of his delay in acquiring many of the skills of the normal child, including the use of language. Because of the severe limitation on visual experience for this child, he actually is functioning on a retarded level. In a sense, he is mentally retarded in the early years even though the potential for learning, aside from the visual handicaps, may be within normal limits. His "functional retardation" is likely to change considerably if he is given adequate opportunity. From this standpoint, then, he eventually may not be retarded and in this way he differs from the real retardate. Because of inadequate differential diagnosis in the early years, a great many visually handicapped children have been labeled mentally retarded and relegated to situations in which they fail to receive adequate intellectual stimulation and education consistent with their mental potential. Obviously, visual problems of less severity may also interfere with the mentally retarded child's ability to learn. It is extremely important to determine the presence of visual problems in a child who is suspected of having mental retardation, and to correct these defects when possible.

RELATED MEDICAL AND DENTAL PROBLEMS

Usually it is the physician who is first called upon to make an initial evaluation of suspected retardation in the very young child. Parents frequently come to the physician with the concern that the baby seems to be developing poorly or has not learned to roll over or sit up as soon as he should. The physician, like the other specialists, compares the performance of the child with the developmental norms available. As discussed previously, slow rates of physical development and motor control generally are part of the picture of mental retardation. Also there may be structural differences in body proportions, head size, bone age, and the like. In a study of 76 patients with IQ's between 50 and 80 (with an equal number above and below 70) and ranging in age from 2 to 17 years, Lilly-white (58) found that 92 percent of the 76 patients were retarded in motor development from 2 to 5 years; 60 percent were retarded in height; 66 percent in weight; and 80 percent in occipital frontal circumference or head size. These findings are in fairly general agreement with those of many other investigations and clinical observations on the physical growth and development of retarded individuals.

All too often, it seems that once a diagnosis of mental retardation has been made other physical problems are not carefully evaluated. It has already been indicated that a wide range of disease enters into the etiology of mental retardation. Likewise, many illnesses and diseases cause conditions that resemble retardation but actually are not because adequate treatment can change the condition and sometimes eliminate what appears to be mental retardation. One of the problems mentioned previously is cerebral palsy, which is another type of specific brain damage causing a multiple array of difficulties that may result in functional or actual retardation. Studies (12) (30) have shown that 50 to 75 percent of the cerebral-palsied population are retarded, but it is important to evaluate each child individually and to separate slow mental functioning from poor motor control.

Many children who are retarded have convulsions that result from another specific kind of brain damage. Convulsions may be present, however, without retardation, or they may result in what appears to be retardation. When a child experiences severe epileptic seizures, for example, such convulsions may interfere with his patterns of normal living to the extent that he is excluded from the kind of stimulation that is needed to develop mentally at a normal rate. It is important that the possibility of convulsions be recognized early and carefully treated if they exist.

The importance of adequate evaluation by the physician of all conditions frequently associated with mental retardation cannot be overstressed. At the same time, the mentally retarded child also is entitled to regular medical care for immunizations, the usual childhood illnesses, the frequent upper respiratory infections to which he is prone, and prompt and complete treatment of such conditions as otitis media. Any chronic and recurrent diseases and illnesses can limit the range of a child's experience and result in subnormal intellectual functioning.

A great deal of the burden of evaluation and management in the early months and years of a child's life will depend upon the physician, particularly the pediatrician. It is essential, then, that he be a member of the diagnostic team that deals with mental retardation. Certainly, it is obvious that the numerous conditions that may be part of mental retardation call for several different medical specialists as part of the diagnostic team if adequate differentiation is to be made.

Few books discuss the dental needs of the retarded child. Yet parents often report that they are unable to obtain the routine dental care for the retarded child that is readily available for other children in the family. It seems that many dentists feel they cannot control the behavior of the mentally retarded child and insist on using anesthesia if they do any dental work. In the program at the University of Oregon Medical School, dental work has been done on retarded children with no adverse effects and little or no difficulty in controlling behavior. The dental hygiene often is quite poor because of the poor movement patterns of the tongue (which would ordinarily remove food particles from the teeth) as well as poor motor control for using a toothbrush. It is recommended that every child who is retarded have regular and thorough dental evaluations, with restorative work done as needed.

INTELLECTUAL FUNCTIONING

Psychologists themselves have been among the foremost in advocating more extensive evaluation than simply giving intelligence tests. Although they have great responsibility for determining the level of intellectual functioning at every age level, results of such testing have been found to be more stable after the child reaches the age of 3. Most psychologists prefer to test a child of any age more than one time before concluding that a given level of mental functioning is the actual potential level of that child.

Robinson and Robinson (76) list three major reasons for the stability and success of psychological testing; it is worthwhile for all involved in diagnosis of the retarded child to be aware of them. (1) The test results have been regarded as samples of behavior that are useful only to the extent that they are proved to be related to or predictive of important behavior outside the test situation. (2) Psychological testing has been carefully standardized in terms of adminstration and scoring procedures. This allows the responses of one child to be compared with those of another or with his own at another time. (3) Meaningful norms have been established for intelligence tests by giving such tests to large numbers of children at each age level. This provides known criteria against which to compare a specific performance.

Although intelligence tests are by far the best standardized psychological measurements, there are many other instruments that can help in one's evaluation of many other aspects of psychological functioning. Such instruments are able to contribute much information about the individual's social achievements, his personal adjustment techniques, his behavioral patterns in specific kinds of situations, and perceptual motor functioning. According to Michal-Smith (69):

One of the prime responsibilities of the clinical psychologist today is to help bring forth the primary causes of mental and social inadequacies and difficulties and to establish with growing clarity the vast network of relationships between these causes and the developmental phenomena of perceptual organization, neurophysiological growth, and the dynamism of behavior, communication, and personality.

In recent years, psychologists have been called upon to give increasing attention to the role that environment plays in intellectual development. Much attention has been called to the socially deprived child and to families without adequate economic opportunity. It has been maintained by many that children in these substandard cultural and social conditions show a pseudomental retardation that responds to adequate opportunity to learn. Many explanations have been made for this phenomenon. Perhaps the most consistent is the two-pronged explanation that intelligence tests are strongly influenced by cultural patterns and that children in the lower socioeconomic groups have less opportunity for the full development of intellectual capacity because of inferior educational opportunities throughout their lives, both in school and in families. It seems likely that because of this situation, the motivation for intellectual attainment is inadequate.

Many individuals with this kind of background continue to function at a subnormal capacity throughout life. The diagnostic importance in this situation is that, while it may be true that extremely deprived sociocultural environments apparently can result in reduced mental capacity or mental development, such need not always be the case. The intellectually and socially deprived individual who is functioning at a retarded level may well have intellectual capacity for normal or above-normal achievement. This capacity must somehow be discovered by the diagnostic team so that steps may be taken to correct the condition if it is possible to do so. Environmental deprivation also has adverse effects on the child who is "truly" retarded to begin with. Such a child is less able to cope with the adverse factors in his environment than if he had normal capacity, so the resultant depressed functioning is compounded.

COMMUNICATION

An individual's ability to communicate with other persons and with himself holds many clues regarding levels of development. A later chapter deals in depth with the problem of evaluating communication problems, but it is necessary here to discuss some general aspects of communication in relation to differential diagnosis. It is extremely important that the speech pathologist or audiologist evaluating children suspected of being mentally retarded know the normal sequences of speech and language development. One of the most widely used scales of development, that of Arnold Gesell and his associates (27), includes limited information on speech and language landmarks. Mecham (68), and Anderson *et al.* (3) provide scales that offer gross guidelines, but the speech pathologist and the audiologist have the responsibility to go beyond these and become well acquainted with the prelanguage activities of children.

Adequate understanding of the early language activities will allow evaluations to be performed on children who are functioning at the 3- or 4-month level of prelanguage skills. Unfortunately, very few speech pathologists or other specialists have discovered the value of this aspect of diagnosis, primarily because they are not aware that specific levels can be established in preverbal language behavior and in very early response to verbalizing and verbal usage.

The speech pathologist also has responsibility for evaluating the oral structures of children in terms of their adequacy to function for speaking. Many deviations have been noted and it is important to be aware of them. It is not unusual for the retarded child to have a short soft palate that results in inadequate palatopharyngeal closure. Submucous cleft palate also is seen frequently. Tongue movements often are gross and may be immature. Malocclusion, particularly open bite, is quite common and appears to be associated with tongue-thrust swallow, thumb sucking, mouth breathing, and a number of other habits. These conditions are not necessarily related to speech problems, but their presence should be noted and if a relationship to the speech problem does exist, the condition should be alleviated if possible.

It should be remembered in connection with differential diagnosis in mental retardation that there are a large number of speech, hearing, and language disorders that can give the appearance of mental retardation and frequently lead to misdiagnosis, misplacement, and mistreatment of a child. The speech of the child with cleft palate or cerebral palsy sometimes leads to the supposition that there is mental retardation. Even the child who stutters frequently has been labeled as retarded. Severe speech delay from any cause certainly creates a condition that gives the appearance of mental retardation, and this delay may occur from a great variety of conditions. The situation is especially likely to be misinterpreted when the communication difficulty is in the comprehension area, such as in receptive aphasia and severe hearing loss. To guard against misdiagnosis and mislabeling, the speech pathologist and the audiologist are essential in the diagnostic process. It is important that information gained in speech, hearing, and language evaluations be made available to the other specialists who are evaluating the other aspects of the total picture of mental retardation.

The diagnostic team

From the above discussion it becomes obvious that diagnosis of mental retardation is no simple task, and certainly is not the province of any one or two specialists. In spite of this fact, however, diagnosis is frequently made on the basis of results of one or two intelligence tests, with very little additional information about the child being available. This certainly is far from adequate in view of the many differential aspects that are involved.

Ideally, the diagnostic team for the mentally retarded would include at least three medical specialists: a pediatrician, a neurologist, and a psychiatrist. Available also should be the consulting services of an endocrinologist, otolaryngologist, ophthalmologist, geneticist, and perhaps some others in special cases. The nonmedical specialists should include the psychologist, speech pathologist, audiologist, social worker, pedodontist, and the teacher if the child is in school. Physical and occupational therapists also can contribute greatly to the diagnostic workup if they are oriented toward evaluation of specific motor age levels and activities of daily living.

Unfortunately, few schools or other centers for the retarded have the services of this many specialists available, but certainly before a child is finally diagnosed as mentally retarded, he should have been thoroughly examined and the findings should have been discussed mutually by at least a pediatrician, a psychologist, a social worker, a speech pathologist, an audiologist, and the teacher if one is involved.

Summary

The speech pathologist who is called upon to evaluate the communication and perhaps provide therapy for a "mentally retarded" child has a right to expect that an adequate diagnostic workup has been completed, with the results being available for his use. He should not be willing to accept what may appear to be too-limited a diagnosis. Information relative to the physical, intellectual, emotional, and environmental status of the mentally retarded individual with whom the speech pathologist is to work has important ramifications in shaping the plan for communication management.

From the above discussion, the importance of all members of the diagnostic team working together for the good of the retarded child should be evident. Diagnosis of such a complex problem calls for the best combined skills of many professionals—and even then the diagnosis of mental retardation is a tremendous job.

Supplemental references

Adler, S. *The Non-Verbal Child*. Springfield, Ill., Charles C Thomas, 1964. Pp. 50–74.

Dameron, L. E. "Development of Intelligence of Infants with Mongolism." *Child Development,* Vol. 34, No. 3, 1963. Pp. 733–738.

Frisina, D. R. "Differential Diagnosis." In Daley, W. T. *Speech and Language Therapy with the Brain-Damaged Child.* Washington, D.C., The Catholic University of America Press, 1962. Pp. 48–79.

Goda, S., and Belver C. Griffith. "Spoken Language of Adolescent Retardates and Its Relation to Intelligence, Age, and Anxiety." *Child Development,* Vol. 33, No. 3, 1962. Pp. 489–498.

Historical Perspective on Mental Retardation During the Decade 1954–1964. Children's Bureau Publication No. 426, 1964. U. S. Government Printing Office, Washington, D.C.

Jordan, T. E. *The Mentally Retarded.* Columbus, Ohio, Charles E. Merrill Books, 1961. Pp. 107–177.

Kephart, N. C. *The Slow-Learning Child in the Classroom.* Columbus, Ohio, Charles E. Merrill Books, 1960.

Koch, R., Nancy Ragsdale, and Betty Gralicker. "A Longitudinal Study of 143 Mentally Retarded Children." *Training School Bulletin,* Vol. 60, 1963. Pp. 4–12.

Panel Discussion. "Mental Retardation: Teamwork in Case Finding, Diagnosis, Approach to Parents, and Guidance." *Journal of Pediatrics,* Vol. 50, No. 2, 1957. Pp. 240–250.

Richards, B. "Mental Retardation: Methods of Diagnosis and Some Recently Described Syndromes." *Canadian Medical Association Journal,* Vol. 89, 1963. Pp. 1024–1029.

The Mentally Retarded Child: A Guide to Services of Social Agencies. Children's Bureau Publication No. 404, 1963. U. S. Government Printing Office, Washington, D.C.

CHAPTER *4*

Medical–dental management of the retarded child

As has been pointed out before, there are a large number of diseases, illnesses, and other conditions that can damage the organism and may result in mental retardation. The mechanisms by which mental retardation occurs from many diseases and illnesses are not clearly defined, but it is known that damage to the brain in many cases causes retardation. Other conditions, such as severe dental anomalies, while hardly resulting in destruction of brain cells, can still produce such an adverse effect on the organism that it is impossible for it to function adequately. Although it cannot be known at the time of their appearance that such conditions positively will result in mental retardation, the fact that they *can* produce this result is an important one.

53

It is known that many illnesses, diseases, dental anomalies, and conditions surrounding them can be prevented, so that medical and dental management for the retarded individual rests basically on a program of prevention— followed by early recognition when the condition has not been prevented, and treatment when possible. It is important that the speech pathologist and audiologist be acquainted with the various illnesses, diseases, dental anomalies, and surrounding conditions that may result in mental retardation and that certainly must be part of the total diagnostic and therapeutic processes if progress is to be maximum.

Wortis (93) states:

> Mental retardation is not the dead-end product of an immutable state. Since brain cells, once destroyed, cannot be regenerated, there are serious limits to our medical help, but, even within these limits, much can be done, and fortunately the destroyed brain cells are seldom the only factors we are called upon to treat.

A great deal of research, experimentation, and clinical effort have gone into the medical treatment not so much of the destroyed brain cells as the physical conditions surrounding the destruction of the brain cells and, more importantly, those conditions likely to cause such destruction.

A number of conditions known to cause mental retardation (but which can be prevented) are listed by Levenson and Bigler (56). These conditions include problems surrounding pregnancy, prematurity, postmaturity, neonatal factors, and traumatic illness or injury any time after birth. While it is not the province of this book to go into detail with respect to these conditions, it is important that they be reviewed briefly.

Prenatal factors

Unfortunately, prenatal factors are the most frequent cause of retardation, yet they are the most difficult to deal with. Less is known about many aspects of such problems, prevention is difficult or impossible, and treatment is often hampered by failure to recognize the condition early enough. In many cases, treatment procedures are not yet known.

METABOLIC DEFECTS

A number of biochemical disorders have been recognized and are becoming increasingly important as known causes of mental retardation. Principal among these defects are phenylketonuria, maple-syrup urine disease (an amino acid urea accompanied by excretion of branch-chained amino acids and mental retardation), galactosemia, cretinism, histidinemia, hyperglycemia, and a number of others of relative infrequency. Unfortunately, few of these diseases are preventable, except by recognizing the eugenic factors that may be involved and by effectively counseling parents. Some of these defects are treatable, however, only to the point that mental retardation may be prevented if the condition is recognized early enough and treatment is effective. Three of these conditions—phenyl-ketonuria, maple-syrup urine disease, and galactosemia—if recognized early enough, can be treated effectively with diet management. Even cretinism, if treated with appropriate amounts of thyroid hormone in the early stages, can undergo considerable physical and mental improvement.

CHROMOSOMAL ABNORMALITIES

Much has been known for some time about chromosomal abnormalities and their effect on mental retardation. Most attention has been given to the condition called mongolism (Down's syndrome), but more recently a number of other chromosomal abnormalities have been discovered and directly related to mental retardation. The means for direct prevention of these conditions is as yet unknown, but a great deal of progress is being made in the field of genetics by way of determining the nature of the chromosomal abnormalities; thus parental counseling concerning these conditions and their management can be of help.

GENETIC DEFECTS

Certain types of retardation are related to genetic factors. Here again the geneticist plays an important role in careful evaluation, which may determine whether such factors play a role in certain families in which retardation is present. The nature of genetic transmission generally is known, and the percentage of risk can be determined on the basis of the nature of the genetic situation. It is known that hydrocephalus, for example, frequently is caused by stenosis of the aqueduct of Sylvius, which is transmitted genetically. Possible surgical treatment of hydrocephalus (by removing cerebral spinal fluid) does not always result in removal of the danger of brain damage. The principle resource of the physician dealing with genetic abnormalities is one of parental counseling, by way of providing information relative to further genetic transmission of conditions causing mental retardation.

OTHER PRENATAL FACTORS

Among other prenatal factors that may result in retardation are diabetes mellitus, myasthenia gravis, and hypothyroidism. Infants born to diabetic mothers have a higher morbidity and mortality rate and a higher incidence of congenital anomalies and brain abnormality than those born of nondiabetic mothers. As diabetes can be well controlled, it is imperative that medical treatment be available to the diabetic mother during pregnancy. Likewise, hypothyroidism can be treated adequately and possible congenital malformation and retardation can be prevented if the condition is treated during pregnancy.

Another factor that fortunately is receiving increasing attention from physicians is that of medication given to the mother during pregnancy. It is known that many types of medication administered to the mother during pregnancy may adversely affect the fetus. The obvious prevention for this situation is very sparing use of medication during pregnancy, especially during the critical first trimester.

Infections during the prenatal period are also an important factor in producing brain damage in the fetus. One of the most important of these is rubella, which has long been recognized as a cause of multiple handicaps—including mental retardation and deafness. The 1964 "epidemic" in the United States has demonstrated that the effects of rubella are serious, and it is still a disease that demands much attention and careful study. Horstman (38) estimated that at least several thousand children were born with major congenital defects and probably many more with less severe handicaps as a result of this epidemic. Unfortunately, there is not yet a known prevention for rubella except early exposure to the virus before child-bearing age, and recovery from it. Eventually, a vaccine probably will be developed to protect individuals from rubella.

Many other infections might be mentioned, among which would be acute bacterial infection that results generally in prematurity, tuberculosis, influenza, polio-myelitis, chickenpox, mumps, measles, and many of the nonspecific viral infections of the upper respiratory system. Prevention is possible in most of these diseases if they are recognized and treated early enough.

Another factor thought to cause damage to the fetus is excessive radiation from exposure to x-ray. The exact amount of radiation that will cause damage to the fetus has not been determined. In view of this risk, the obvious preventive aspect is avoidance of x-ray during any period of pregnancy, if possible.

Perinatal factors

Many events can occur during the birth period to cause damage that will result in mental retardation. It is known that a very high correlation exists between prematurity and brain damage. In fact, prematurity is highly correlated with a large number of congenital abnormalities. G. K. Döring (17) in a 1965 study in Germany found that premature infants showed three to four times more malformations than term infants, and contributed 60 to 70 percent of the total number of neonatal deaths. This study and many others have pointed out that prematurity also is associated with poor socioeconomic status as well as with prenatal disease factors.

Other commonly known causes of damage during the natal period are neonatal asphyxia and delivery complications that may lead to hemorrhage around the brain, head injury, or suffocation that may result in severe damage. An important area of possible damage is that of hemolytic disease of the newborn. This is a condition which results from Rh incompatibility in the mother and if not treated may result in kernicterus, high-frequency deafness, and/or mental retardation, among other disorders.

Preventive measures are possible in most of these conditions. Careful prenatal care of the mother may reduce prematurity and special care during the birth process and the neonatal period may prevent damage. Treatment of the Rh-negative mother has been standard procedure for some time, with early transfusion of the newborn baby being perhaps the most common practice.

Postnatal factors

The newborn child and the growing child are subject to many kinds of infections, as well as accidents and poisons that may have a traumatic effect that results in brain damage and mental retardation. Bacterial meningitis, tuberculosis meningitis, and viral encephalitis often show neurologic damage that may result in retardation. Recently there has been increasing awareness of the "battered child syndrome," which appears in children who have been beaten severely by their parents or guardians—with resulting head injury. Enough concern over this situation has been generated that many states now have laws requiring suspected cases of child mistreatment to be reported by physicians.

All of these postnatal conditions may be prevented, but many of them are elusive and difficult—especially accidents, poisons, and the battered child. Unfortunately, these conditions, again, are associated more directly with the lower socioeconomic groups, making control more difficult because children in this group are less likely to have frequent contact with physicians or other professional specialists. The alert physician, however, does manage to prevent many of these possible conditions, and the alert citizen must recognize that general social improvement eventually may do a great deal to alleviate them.

Drug therapy

A great deal of experimentation has taken place with the use of various drugs that act as tranquilizing agents or to increase intellectual activity. Both drugs and diet are being used to control body chemistry in an attempt to prevent brain damage. At various times, much hope has been held that certain kinds of drugs would prevent, improve, and even in some highly optimistic experiments cure mental retardation. Among the drugs involved have been thyroid extract, glutamic acid, dexedrine, and various tranquilizers. However, most of the hope for great improvement through drugs has not been justified. Jordan (45) summarizes it this way:

There seems to be reason to believe that the ataraxic drugs can render an individual more accessible to training, but there is little evidence for believing that we have yet developed, or will ever develop, a therapy that will radically alter the status of retardates from intellectual inadequacy to normality.

The chief value to be gained from the use of drugs in treating the mentally retarded is that such agents may make the child more amenable to management and training. Especially valuable in some cases has been the use of drugs to decrease the activity of the hyperactive child; sometimes an increase in attention span results. In a few cases, increased mental activity has been reported from the use of drugs, thus making training more profitable. This result certainly has not been widespread, however, and at present does not hold a great deal of promise. No drug has yet been found that appreciably increases the intelligence of a child. The speech clinician will need to be aware of the fact that parents may well be misled by claims that have been made for drugs in this direction.

Dental management

Dental abnormalities—their recognition, care, and steps for possible prevention—have received very little attention in connection with the mentally retarded child. Several reasons may account for this. One is that dental aspects of the retarded child frequently are not different from those of the nonretarded and, therefore, have not received separate consideration. A second more important reason, perhaps, is that the retarded child frequently is much more difficult to treat dentally than the nonretarded, so that parents and dentists both often have avoided necessary dental care.

More frequent recognition of the fact that the retarded child must be in the very best of health if he is to function up to his capacity would make it obvious that dental care is highly important in the management of the retardate. In a few isolated mental retardation centers, increasing attention is being paid to the dental needs of the retarded individual. Information from these centers is making it evident that there are dental problems peculiar to the retarded, and that this aspect does need considerable attention.

It is now known that dental problems among retardates are more prevalent than among the nonretarded. In a study of 99 retarded children at the University of Oregon Medical School's Multi-Discipline Clinic for Retarded Children numerous dental conditions—outlined in Table 6—were reported by Gullickson (31).

These children ranged in age from 5 to 10 years and their intelligence quotients on Stanford Binet or WISC tests were between 10 and 80. Only 5 were classified as severely retarded; the rest were moderately or mildly retarded.

Gullickson (31) also pointed out that the oral cavity plays a vital role in the physiology of the human body and that a child is not healthy if he has deep carious lesions, abscessed teeth, oral infections, or severe malocclusion. The important factor relating to the retardate is that he is perhaps more subject to these problems than the nonretarded, and the effects of these disabilities on him are more severe.

T A B L E 6. DENTAL ABNORMALITIES OF
99 RETARDED CHILDREN

	Percent
Active caries	65
Infected teeth	19
Gingivitis	38
Poor oral hygiene	79
Palatal deviations	37
Congenitally missing teeth	13
Malformation of teeth	24
Malocclusions	69
No previous dental care	55

SOURCE: J. Gullickson. "Dental Diagnosis and Treatment of Mentally Retarded Children." Unpublished paper, University of Oregon Medical School, Portland, Oregon, 1966. P. 6.

It is obvious that all of the above-mentioned dental problems may have been prevented except for the palatal abnormalities, the missing teeth, and the malformations. All of the conditions are treatable, however, and this is an important consideration among the retarded.

As suggested previously, one of the major problems in the dental management of the retarded child is that he may be more difficult to control than the nonretarded. Gullickson (31) indicates that he has found that once a child reaches the mental age of 2 years he usually can be conditioned or taught to accept most dental procedures. He did find, however, that sedation was necessary in proportion to the severity of the retardation. It is obvious, too, that the more severe the retardation the less possibility there is of a child's being able to wear and care for a space maintainer, a speech appliance, or some other prosthetic device. In his work Gullickson (31) constructed appliances for 4 children who had hypernasal voice quality. All of these devices were worn successfully and produced favorable results. One child with an IQ of 30 accepted and tolerated his appliance especially well.

Of primary concern to the speech pathologist and audiologist are the oral malformations, palatal deviations, malocclusions, and conditions of acute dental distress. These disorders have been discussed in an earlier chapter, but it is obvious that close working relationships between the dentist and the speech pathologist are highly important in the over-all management of communication problems of the retarded population. Dental problems such as those mentioned often interfere with speech improvement; yet these are problems that can be corrected. The child in distress from dental infection or just plain toothache is not likely to respond adequately to any testing or therapeutic procedure, including speech therapy. The services of a dentist might well change the child's entire performance, and this avenue should not be overlooked.

General health aspects

There still is considerable disagreement with respect to the possibility of improving a child's intelligence. The answer to this question depends on how narrowly one defines intelligence and mental retardation. If we accept the premise that there is a true retardation based on destruction of or a limited number of adequately functioning brain cells, and if we assume that intelligence tests measure these conditions with reasonable accuracy, then the conclusion that intelligence cannot be changed seems to be valid. If, on the other hand, there are conditions related to the child's physical or mental health that seriously disrupt his functioning, these conditions should receive attention.

The many other factors surrounding the mentally retarded child, as with any other individual, may and frequently do prevent his functioning according to his capabilities. That is, the mentally retarded child frequently functions considerably below his mental age in many areas. A useful basic philosophy in the management of the retarded child is that he should be in the best possible physical and mental health in order to function to his potential. This is true for any child, but in the case of the retardate it is especially important because he has so much against him anyway. In addition to this, he is less capable of adapting to or compensating for additional defects and problems. Treatment to bring the retarded child's functioning up to his capacity is vitally needed.

A description of medical–dental diagnostic and treatment procedures used in one clinic at the University of Oregon Medical School is presented here as a possible model for providing information to help retarded children function at top capacity. In the Multi-Discipline Clinic (13), medical evaluation includes a complete history and physical examination by a pediatrician. Each child is given an eye examination and hearing assessment. He has multiple laboratory studies as follow: (1) electroencephalogram, awake and asleep; (2) routine urinalysis; (3) urinary amino-acid determination; (4) stool examination; (5) complete radiographic survey; (6) medical photography; (7) blood chemistry; (8) hematology; and (9) karyotyping procedures. Additional medical examinations and studies are performed by the appropriate specialists when indicated.

A week's diet diary is kept for the child prior to his admission. This record is analyzed by a dietician for total caloric nutrient, vitamin, and mineral content. Complete occupational and physical therapy testing is provided; this includes an assessment of functional ability and various motor skills and activities used in daily living. It often establishes a baseline from which parents and therapists begin specific training.

The dental evaluation includes a complete oral evaluation by visual inspection, intraoral and lateral jaw radiographs, and plaster casts of the dentition. Also, as a diagnostic procedure, a prophylaxis is provided each child to assess his reaction to simple procedures. A sodium floride treatment is given to those who have not received one in the past year.

In this program the child receives psychological appraisal, including long-term behavioral observation. He also has audiological assessment as well as speech and language examinations that establish levels of verbal comprehension, verbal communication, articulation ability and intelligibility. Descriptions of speech or language disorders and physical findings that might relate to language abilities are provided for all specialists evaluating the child.

The above diagnostic procedures take place during a

4-week period, in which 10 children at a time attend daily diagnostic and observation sessions. Concurrent with these examinations and observations, parents are required to attend a number of individual and group-instruction counseling sessions.

Whatever medical and dental problems are found to be present are treated during the diagnostic period or afterwards as the need may indicate. A very important aspect is in the counseling sessions with parents, in which medical and dental instruction is given. If appropriate, these sessions include genetic counseling. The various specialists are under the direction of a pediatrician, but all disciplines function together as a diagnostic and management team.

Summary

From the above description it will be seen that, ideally, medical and dental management of the retarded child is a multidiscipline procedure and can no more be done in isolation by any one or two persons than can the other diagnostic or therapeutic processes. The importance of the medical–dental aspects to the speech pathologist and audiologist have been pointed out. The importance of establishing good working relationships among medical–dental specialists, speech and hearing specialists, psychologists, education specialists, and others becomes obvious. The communication specialist can be a key person in establishing such relationships.

Supplemental references

Caplan, G. *Prevention of Mental Disorders in Children: Initial Explorations.* New York, Basic Books, 1961.

Deisher, R. W. "Role of the Physician in Maintaining Continuity of Care and Guidance." *Journal of Pediatrics,* Vol. 50, No. 2, 1957. Pp. 231–235.

Jervis, G. A. "Medical Aspects of Mental Retardation." *Journal of Rehabilitation,* Vol. 28, No. 6, 1962. Pp. 34–36.

Kugel, R. B., and J. Mohr. "Mental Retardation and Physical Growth." *American Journal of Mental Deficiency,* Vol. 68, No. 1, 1963. Pp. 41–48.

LaVeck, G. D., and F. de la Cruz. "Medical Advances in Prevention of Mental Retardation." In Hellmuth, J., ed., *The Special Child in Century 21.* Seattle, Wash., 1964. Pp. 23–46.

Marinus, C. J. "Physical Factors in Mental Retardation." *Exceptional Children,* Vol. 20, No. 3, 1953. Pp. 124–131.

Yannett, Herman. "Research in the Field of Mental Retardation." *Journal of Pediatrics,* Vol. 50, No. 2, 1957. Pp. 236–239.

CHAPTER 5

Educational management

Educational procedures for all children have changed remarkably in the last 20 years, and educational management for the mentally retarded is no exception. The continual movement toward urbanization and mechanization has placed additional and different demands on the schools. The need to produce educated individuals who are creative and adaptable enough to change with the new technological developments is difficult to meet with students of normal intelligence; it is almost impossible with mentally retarded students. On the other hand, failure to meet the demands increases the number of individuals for whom society must find some means of support.

The need for basic abilities in reading, writing, and arithmetic has increased to the extent that employment without these skills is almost nonexistent. As the number of jobs available to individuals who do not possess such skills continues to decrease, it becomes more necessary that schools find ways of developing these basic skills in the retarded child. Much exploration of different methodology in teaching, much reasearch into the nature of learning, and assistance from newer fields of technology are being utilized in efforts effectively to teach and train mentally retarded individuals.

Another trend that affects the educational programs of the schools and institutions is the tendency for more and more retarded individuals to live at home. This increases the need for day schools, day care centers, and special classes. Related to this is the fact that the level of intelligence of individuals living in institutions is lower now than it was 20 years ago. Beyond doubt, more retardates living at home also reflects greater acceptance of deviant individuals by society in general. The need for institutional care has not decreased because the number of retarded individuals has increased along with the increase in the general population.

With these changes in focus toward retardates, questions arise as to what such people can be taught, what kinds of occupations and other activities they can be directed toward, and what kinds of communication skills they need. We do not have definite answers to these questions at the present time, but there is much speculation as to how much and what can be taught retarded individuals in the educable and trainable groups.

It generally has been assumed that those mentally retarded individuals classed as "educable" can acquire limited academic skills, such as reading, writing, and basic arithmetic processes. The majority of them, as adults, blend into society at large, being self-supporting socially and economically. Jobs may range from managerial to unskilled labor positions, although most of the men work as laborers and the women as housekeepers. It has been suggested that the success or failure in work situations is related to work-habit variables such as initiative, self-confidence, cooperation, cheerfulness, and respect for the supervisor. Speech and language skills often are considered adequate, but rudeness, vulgarity, and lack of cheerfulness have been mentioned as deficiencies of the mildly retarded group.

Those classed as "trainable" are more open to question with regard to employment. It was assumed for a long time that individuals with an IQ below 50 could profit very little from academic instruction, and this still is the belief of many professionals in the field. This feeling may result in part from the early assumption on the part of some educators that the retarded individual should learn (albeit at a slower rate) the same academic material if he is taught in the traditional manner. Recently educators have given considerable attention to the trainable group in response to increasing demands on the schools to provide academic training for such people. As a result, experimentation with modified methods of teaching skills and information needed in activities of daily living has resulted in reports of more success. Currently, however, less than half of this group work for pay in the community.

Some use public transportation adequately. Almost half, if living at home, give regular help with useful tasks. Most are capable of conversation that usually is limited to talking about the immediate surroundings.

It is likely that the "custodial" group can profit little from any formalized instruction and, for the most part, will be entirely dependent even for personal care. A few can achieve some self-help skills, but frequently they do not achieve even this level. Language skills usually are limited to vocalization to attract attention, and sometimes to one or two words.

Whatever the level of retardation, the child will reach his potential only if the various aspects of his total learning environment are utilized to the fullest extent. The over-all management of the retarded child then becomes of paramount importance.

Home instruction

In most cases of retardation, parents prefer to keep the child at home as long as possible. Consideration of the home situation in regard to the education of the retarded child is an important one because the early years of life are critical for learning in the retarded child as well as in the nonretarded. Most parents need guidance in terms of when to expect development of interest in books, TV programs, and the other experiences that most children enjoy before formal schooling begins.

Some parents look to their pediatricians for guidance in these matters. Others seek advice from psychologists or speech pathologists with whom they have had contact through diagnostic centers. Most diagnostic teams have accepted responsibility for consultation with parents regarding the early training and education of the retarded child. The management of behavior problems, and discussion of feeding difficulties, toilet training, and speech and language development may require repeated conferences between parents and some professional worker. Adequate training in these areas may require much skill on the part of parents of retarded children.

In addition, it frequently has been said that the retarded child must be taught many things that the normal child learns just by living. Therefore, parents of retarded children must assume much responsibility for teaching about things with which they ordinarily would not be concerned. Educational progress in later years may depend largely upon the foundation established in the home. Parents will make a substantial contribution to their child's educational future if they can succeed in teaching him to attend to things that are to be learned, to follow simple directions, and to develop inquisitiveness regarding things around him. In many cases, however, much more than this can be done.

Home teaching programs

For many reasons, school instruction programs provided in the home are not well established in relation to retarded children. This reflects the large numbers of retarded children, the limited numbers of children who can be served by one teacher, and the expensive nature of this educational endeavor. In some instances, a child is unable to leave his home because of physical limitations such as uncontrolled seizures or heart problems. Home instruction is provided for such retarded children just as it would be for the nonretarded. This type of educational program for retardates usually is carried out by home teachers trained to work with children who have various handicaps. Such work requires the ability to teach numerous subjects and children of a wide age range. Its success is dependent in large measure on the cooperation of parents in providing a quiet room for the instruction, helping select the time when the child is usually most alert, encouraging the child to follow through on assignments, and supplementing instruction with educational television programs, visits from other children, and other appropriate activities. The home teacher and the parents must work together very closely.

School systems seem to be more willing to provide home teachers for children in the educable retarded group than in the trainable group. No doubt part of the reason is related to the expense of the home instruction programs and the widely accepted attitude that the trainable retarded group learns so little in the way of academic skills that the value of a home teacher is highly questionable. Other specialists, such as the public health nurse, may visit the home to consult with parents regularly about development of self-help skills and general activities of daily living. More often, the parents take the child to a clinic or diagnostic center for regular conferences regarding these matters.

In a very few instances, home instruction programs are provided to help parents learn more effective ways of dealing with retarded children in the custodial group. Although quite different from the home instruction programs aimed at teaching academic skills, such programs may be quite helpful to parents. Often it is the public health nurse who visits the home regularly and instructs the parents in ways of teaching the retarded child such self-help activities as he may be capable of learning—attempting toilet training when indicated and exploring various ways of handling the child to make the care as efficient and easy as possible. Occupational and physical therapists sometimes visit homes to teach parents ways to help the child develop methods of locomotion and self-help activities such as eating, dressing, and general principles of motor development.

Although home instruction programs for retardates are not well established and there is little data from which to judge their value, there are indications that such programs are effective in helping retarded children achieve their potential levels of development. As more programs of this nature are developed and more information becomes available on the achievements of such programs, better guidelines will be evident.

When home teaching programs are available for the retarded, they offer many opportunities to develop communication skills. For this to take place, however, the teacher must understand the nature of the communication problems of the retarded, and must make use of the information and techniques for developing better speech and language. Ideally, a speech clinician should be involved in this home program, either directly or by way of assisting the home teacher with information and materials. The school speech clinician should be alert to these possibilities and assist whenever possible.

Preschool educational activities

Many regular nursery schools are willing to accept retarded children and if they are placed in appropriate age groups, they frequently have successful experiences. Placement should be made according to mental age rather than chronological age. Primarily, the values lie in the opportunities to learn to get along with other children, to participate in organized play activities, and to learn to follow directions given to groups. These early learning experiences help to develop self-expression through such things as music, specific play activities, artwork, and communication with other members of the group. The retarded child may learn to play cooperatively with other children and become as independent as his current level of development allows. Physical coordination may be improved through the games the children play. Activities such as riding a tricycle, hopping, skipping, running, and jumping, as well as mastery of finer motor skills, usually are especially valuable for the retarded and are available in good nursery schools. The systematic guidance of nursery school teachers often provides opportunities for learning that are not available at home. Other children at the nursery school often find ways of showing the retarded child how to do things that would never occur to the parents or teachers.

Privately sponsored centers for the retarded often provide care and training for groups of retarded pre-school children. Frequently they are sponsored by the local and state associations for retarded children, and employ reasonably well-trained teachers. These facilities are for both trainable and educable levels of retarded children and provide basically the same curriculum and training for retarded children as for the younger non-retarded child. Such facilities, when available, frequently are a wise choice of placement for the retarded child of 5, 6, or 7 years of age. Most special classes in public schools cannot accept children younger than 8 years, but the time before this stage also should be used for learning; private centers often fill this gap in educational facilities. When such programs are not available, the Head Start programs designed for culturally deprived or disadvantaged children may provide a program that is worthwhile for the retarded child. Some of the Head Start programs have utilized teaching techniques that have proved quite successful with retarded children.

Special classes

According to the 1967 President's Committee on Mental Retardation (25), approximately half of the nation's 25,000 school districts offer special classes for students who have difficulty learning. Of these facilities, 43,525 classes serve 587,722 educable retarded children and another 8,522 classes include 89,252 trainable retarded students. Teachers in these classes have similar objectives for their pupils as do teachers in regular classrooms; that is, the goal of each child's achieving and learning all that he has the ability to learn. However, the schools must continue to develop and use educational methodology that will make it possible for the retarded child to become socially adequate and economically productive in a society that changes rapidly.

Most of the special classes mentioned above are in public schools. Along with them, additional classes are available in private residential schools and private day schools; many mildly retarded children continue in regular classrooms. For those remaining in regular classrooms, the pace often is too rapid and failures are more frequent. It has been suggested that much of the lack of motivation described as part of the behavior of the retarded child may be a result of the inability to function adequately in regular classroom settings. The mildly retarded or educable retardates in particular recognize their failures and are very much aware of their own intellectual limitations. Their frustrations are seen frequently in the form of temper tantrums, sullenness, inattentiveness, or unwillingness to attempt tasks. If expectations are in keeping with abilities of the retarded child, much of this frustration can be eliminated and the student will be free to learn at the level of his ability.

It generally is accepted that the educable group of retarded children can be expected to achieve academic skills in reading, writing, mathematics, and language ranging from second- through about fifth-grade levels. The achievement of these academic skills is governed by the rate of mental development and does not correspond with chronological age. The rate of achievement also follows the rate of mental development—so that if the child is gaining 8 months of mental age in 12 months of chronological age, he is likely to achieve about 6 months of academic progress in one 9-month school year. Such achievement presupposes that the instructional methods are adequate, that students are given sufficient recognition for their accomplishments, and that physical health and home environment are favorable.

One of the distinct advantages of the special classes is that they usually are small. In most instances, a primary-class enrollment will range between 8 and 12. This provides considerable opportunity for the well-trained teacher to work with each child at his particular level of ability and to move ahead at the right pace for each child in all academic subjects taught. Small classes also provide more time and opportunity to emphasize social competency and personal adequacy. In the younger age levels, much effort should be directed toward these objectives so that social problems will not interfere with training of occupational skills at later age levels.

Frequently the teacher must develop materials for reading and arithmetic that are based on the personal experiences of the students. The books that are appropriate for the level of achievement of the retarded child may not contain subject matter of interest to him. Some books developed for remedial reading instruction may be quite appropriate, but much material will need to be designed for individual children and small groups in a given special class. Usually, retarded children do not generalize their responses to appropriate situations; therefore, much more activity in transferring newly acquired knowledge to various situations may be needed. This will involve actual and simulated situations that may be used to help build good habits of health, safety, and work along with the academic skill.

Special classes at the secondary level (junior and senior high school) are becoming more prevalent as communities and school systems provide continued education for students from special classes in elementary school. The major goal of such classes is to provide the necessary preparation for the retarded individual to take his place in society and to function as independently as his level of ability allows. The classes may be a little larger, but usually will have no more than 18 or 20 students per class.

The specific nature of instruction in secondary classes for retarded children varies with the class. Generally, emphasis on the practical use of academic subjects receives considerable attention. Reading may be done from newspapers, telephone directories, cookbooks, instructions for operating common household tools, grocery store labels, and driver's manuals. Practice in such domestic skills as cooking, sewing, and child care may be provided for girls, while the boys participate in activities such as household mechanics, automobile repair, and electrical and metal work.

Many school systems have made arrangements with employers in the community to provide part-time work–learning opportunities for retarded students. Such situations provide excellent means of developing good work habits of punctuality, pride in completed tasks, personal habits that encourage acceptance by others, and ability to follow directions. Acquisition of such aspects of personal adjustment increases the retarded individual's sense of personal worth and social belonging as well as the probability that he will obtain and maintain a job for pay after he finishes school.

Telford and Sawry (86) have summarized the broad education and training objectives for the mentally retarded as being: (1) adequate social development; (2) academic achievement to ability level; (3) the development of vocational skill; (4) personal habits and adjustments satisfactory to society and to individuals. Much progress has been made toward the attainment of such goals within the setting of special classes in regular and private schools. However, if schools are to keep pace with our rapidly changing world, we need continued improvement in instructional quality and methodology as well as in the application of research findings to the education of mentally retarded students.

Probably most of the school systems that offer special classes for the retarded also provide speech and language therapy for these classes. Any school speech clinician may expect assignment to this kind of situation. For this reason he should understand the nature of the special programs so that his work will be as effective as possible. (The chapters that follow provide general and specific procedures that will apply to such situations.)

Institutional instructional programs

Many changes have been demonstrated in the institutional programs for severely retarded children requiring custodial care. Even though the 1967 President's Committee on Mental Retardation (25) states that three-quarters of the nation's 201,000 institutionalized mentally retarded live in buildings 50 years old or more, and that many of the buildings were not designed for purposes of housing retardates, there are encouraging signs. More attention is being given to the design of new buildings and to the functional use of existing buildings. More important, however, is the increasing confidence that many individuals in the severely retarded group can learn some self-help skills. More and more state institutions are providing instructional staff to explore the methodology and effectiveness of various techniques for training these severely handicapped individuals.

The use of operant conditioning in the teaching of the severely retarded has demonstrated that many retardates in custodial care situations, both private and state-supported, probably can be trained to care for their own toilet needs, feed themselves, and vocalize when they need help. Hollis and Gorton (35) summarize much of the work that has been done in training severely retarded children in the areas of behavior, gross perceptual motor skills, imitation of various motor behaviors, and self-care tasks. These authors suggest that the principles of behavioral engineering provide the operational procedures necessary to develop training programs for the custodial group of retardates long considered incapable of learning.

More and more evidence accumulates that the manipulation of contingencies and consequences by the staff caring for the severely retarded individual can and does bring about changes in his behavior. The extent to which these methods of training can change the lives of the large number of severely retarded is not yet known. Certainly these methods deserve further consideration and use to permit evaluation of their lasting results and impact on the functioning level of institutional populations.

It will be remembered that more and more retarded individuals are living at home and not in institutions. Those living in institutions are more severely handicapped mentally and physically, so that the goals of the educational programs in institutions must continually be shifted in keeping with the abilities of the population. In addition to this factor, many of the retardates living in institutions have additional handicaps such as cerebral palsy, deafness, or blindness. These additional handicaps make educational goals and training more limited. The need for custodial care will continue to exist even if much is accomplished in training severely retarded individuals.

In spite of the generally lower level of abilities of institutionalized retardates, many of these individuals possess abilities that justify training in communication skills. (This kind of training is discussed in the following chapters.)

Summary

Educational planning should begin as soon as the diagnosis of retardation has been made. For some children, such as those with Down's syndrome, this should occur within a few weeks after birth. Others will not be identified until after they start regular school. Adequate management of educational needs involves cooperative planning among parents, medical specialists, psychologists, and speech and hearing specialists.

Educational needs of the retarded child continue to change as the cultural and technical aspects of our society change, and it is essential to plan in terms of what our world may be like when the retarded child is an adult, rather than in terms of our present situation. Naturally, this is not entirely possible; but to the extent that changes are predictable, it is important to consider them.

The home, preschool, special schools, special classes in regular schools, and institutions all have important roles to fulfill in meeting the educational needs of retarded children. Coordination of efforts in these various settings is important. Careful selection of educational facilities in view of a particular child's needs is essential if the best educational management is to be followed.

The more severe the retardation, the less likely it is that educational management will enable the child to be a self-sufficient citizen. However, the more self-sufficient each retarded child can become, the less care and support he will demand from the rest of society. In long-range planning, it may prove less expensive to provide educational and training opportunities to develop each retarded child to his maximum capacity for independent functioning than to provide custodial care for large numbers of retardates throughout their life spans.

The role of the speech pathologist and audiologist in educational management should extend much beyond concern for speech and hearing disorders only. Because the inability to communicate adequately is almost universal among the retarded, the specialist in communication is central in the management process. He frequently is in a position to initiate needed care outside of his specialty; he almost always is in a good position to help counsel and guide the parents, and he can be very effective in integrating the efforts of the many disciplines and the many factors involved in adequate educational management.

Supplemental references

Huber, W. G., and A. Z. Soforenko. "Factors Contributing to the Vocational Success or Non-Success of the Institutionalized Retardate." *The Training School Bulletin,* Vol. 60, No. 1, 1963. Pp. 43–51.

Indorf, F. A. "Teaching Slow-Learning Children in the Regular Classroom." *Slow Learning Child,* Vol. 10, 1963. Pp. 38–46.

Johnson, G. O. "Education of Mentally Retarded Children." In Cruikshank, W. M., and G. O. Johnson, eds. *Education of Exceptional Children and Youth.* Englewood Cliffs, N.J., Prentice-Hall, 1967. Pp. 194–237.

Kirk, S. A. "Research in Education." In *Mental Retardation,* Stevens, H. A., and R. Heber, eds. Chicago, University of Chicago Press, 1964. Pp. 57–99.

Milgram, N. A., and H. G. Furth. "The Influence of Language on Concept Attainment in Educable Retarded Children." *American Journal of Mental Deficiency,* Vol. 67, 1963. Pp. 733–739.

Peck, J. R., and W. B. Stephens. *Success of Young Adult Male Retardates.* Austin, Texas, University of Texas, 1964.

Reynolds, M. C. "The Responsibility of School for Trainable Retarded Children." *Exceptional Children,* Vol. 29, No. 1, 1962. Pp. 53–56.

Snyder, E. "Learning Problems, Program Planning, and Curriculum for the Mentally Retarded." In Hellmuth, J., ed., *The Special Child in Century 21.* Seattle, Wash., Special Child Publications of the Seguin School, 1964. Pp. 225–246.

Tisdall, W. J. "Productive Thinking in Retarded Children." *Exceptional Children,* Vol. 29, No. 1, 1962. Pp. 36–41.

Warren, S. A. "Academic Achievement of Trainable Pupils with Five or More Years of Schooling." *The Training School Bulletin,* Vol. 60, No. 2, 1963. Pp. 75–88.

CHAPTER 6

Diagnosis of communication disorders

When dealing with the communication problems of mentally retarded children, it is of primary importance for the speech pathologist to be completely familiar with the significant patterns and sequences of normal speech and language development. Admittedly, much remains to be discovered about how speech and language develop, yet there is much we do know. Without this knowledge it is most difficult to recognize aspects of delay and deviations from average development. It is interesting and unfortunate that a great many speech and hearing training centers fail to provide students with an adequate background in the developmental aspects of speech and language. The result is that the speech diagnostician frequently appears in the field looking for "speech disorders" without a full knowledge of what constitutes a disorder or the standard from which speech or language deviates when it is disordered. With respect to the mentally retarded in particular, but also with all other speech and language problems, the fundamental base for adequate diagnosis must be normal speech and language development. If the speech pathologist does not have this training, several references at the end of this chapter will be helpful.

Many discussions of normal speech and language development neglect the early years of life and tend to start with the skills that normal children exhibit at about 2 to 3 years of age. Many of the more severely mentally retarded children will not develop 2-year language skills until they are 5 or 6 years old chronologically. Therefore, it is important to be aware of the earlier stages of speech and language development. Tests for assessing communication skills in infancy are quite limited and have shown poor reliability as predictors of ultimate achievement. However, they do provide a description of functioning at a given age and aid in counseling parents about the next stage of language development that might be expected.

The importance of the team evaluation in establishing a diagnosis of mental retardation was emphasized in an earlier chapter. In the team situation, the speech pathologist provides a description of speech and language skills that is combined with similar appraisals of physical, emotional, and intellectual behavior; when all appraisals are appropriately synthesized, the diagnosis of mental retardation is possible. However, the speech pathologist also is responsible for using the information provided by other disciplines to develop a differential diagnosis of the communication problems of the mentally retarded individual. In this instance, he must determine the extent to which mental retardation influences the communication deficit and determine the relationship between physical factors and the speech problems. If emotional problems are present, their relationship to the communication abilities of the individual must be assessed. In most instances, some of these relationships will be quite clear, but often a part of the communication problem remains unexplained. These considerations are essential before an adequate plan of management can be developed or any predictions as to the outcome of the communication problem can be made.

The approach to such analysis may be the same in mental retardation as in any other type of communication problem. It should consist of applying the scientific method to all the processes of communication. This method, as reflected by Kempthorne (47), involves observation, abstraction of essentials, application of statistics, prediction of new events, and, after many repetitions of the cycle, formulation of theories. In other words, it is the task of the speech pathologist to discover and describe precisely the aspects of communication in specific conditions, to compare them with "norms," to predict movement from the observed toward the desired norm, to apply techniques that will bring about that movement, then to determine if the prediction was accurate or inaccurate. Separation of diagnosis and management of the communication problem allows presentation of information in an organized manner. However, in practice, diagnosis is an ongoing part of management and occurs during each repetition of the cycle.

Separation of speech and language, as was done in an earlier chapter, also is convenient in terms of presenting information, but the two are closely related and some of the basic processes to be evaluated underlie both. Learning speech and language is an important task for the child because it plays a role in the satisfaction of physiological and psychological needs, provides a means of exploring relationships with people and things, and serves a function in play, self-stimulation, self-regulation, and self-reinforcement.

With an understanding of the scientific methodology, the sequences of normal speech and language development, and the functions that language serves, the speech pathologist and the audiologist are ready to observe, describe, and evaluate the basic processes of respiration, phonation, resonation, articulation, symbolization, and audition. Assessment of the peripheral speech mechanism is important and might best be considered as each part relates to the process being studied. Developmental aspects of each process should be related to the speech and language functions usually acquired at the same age level.

Respiration

Respiration is the process involved in the delivery of oxygen to the constituent cells of an organism and the removal from them of carbon dioxide. It also involves a series of chemical reactions by which energy is made available to cells. These functions are related to life purposes in which inhalation-exhalation cycles are performed in a one-to-one ratio. Respiration also provides the power supply or the energy for speech, and is performed in about a one-to-seven ratio of inhalation to exhalation. The respiration process may be disturbed centrally or peripherally and may involve both inhalation and exhalation.

Maturational aspects of respiration are not well documented, but it is possible to describe some functions. According to Gray and Wise (29), most adults utilize three regions (thoracic, medial, and abdominal), with one of them being predominant. It has been repeatedly observed that most infants use only abdominal breathing. It is thought that the child usually changes from predominantly abdominal breathing to medial breathing around the time that he assumes upright walking and the ribs become more oblique than horizontal. Interestingly enough, this also is about the time when first words are used. For most children these skills develop around 12 months of age, but for children who are mentally retarded this development is delayed from 1 to 3 years, depending on the amount of retardation. Adequate speakers have been observed to use all three types of breathing. However, Gray and Wise (29) point out that clavicular breathing results in more frequent inhalation and less control of exhalation. Thus it is less desirable for speaking purposes than thoracic breathing.

The relationship between posture and respiratory function also should be mentioned. Maintenance of pharyngeal airway has been described by Shelton and Bosma (81) in postpolio patients, and the posture associated with this condition is not unlike that seen in mentally retarded individuals. The awkward humped shoulders and strained positions described by Gray and Wise (29) as contributing to poor respiratory function also may be observed in retardates. Mouth breathing and upper-respiratory infection frequently are reported among mongoloids and other retarded children. The effects of mouth breathing on respiratory function during speech deserves further study, but its close association with high arched palates and tongue-thrust patterns of swallow indicates it is present frequently in such speech problems as lisping.

The following speech problems that are influenced by respiratory function were elaborated on by Darley (16).

1. Speaking on supplemental air, which may result in harshness.

2. Loss of most of the breath supply before phonation, resulting in problems of vocal intensity, phrasing, and possibly articulation.

3. Wasting air, which is sometimes associated with breathy voice quality.

4. Poor breath control, which may contribute to wavering and to a tremulous voice quality.

5. Speaking on inhalation, resulting in poor flow of speech.

6. Inability to direct the breath stream orally and with precision, which may result in various articulation problems—including weakness of many consonants.

Any of the speech problems associated with respiratory dysfunction should alert the speech clinician to observe respiration carefully; if evidence of respiratory dysfunction exists, more extensive study of respiration may be indicated. For example, inability to direct the air stream orally—as observed in retarded children who have palatal insufficiency or palatal paresis—can be studied carefully with cineradiographic techniques. Poor vocal volume may result from loss of breath supply or inadequate breath support. Goddard (28) has provided some norms for children from 5 to 12 years of age that offer a means of comparing oral breath-pressure scores. Her results indicate that children who are unable to impound at least 5 ounces of oral breath pressure demonstrated more articulation errors than those with better scores.

In summary, respiration is the power for producing speech; if this process is inadequate, most of the subsequent stages of speech production are likely to be affected. It should be carefully assessed in relation to the nature of speech problems observed.

Phonation

Phonation involves production of the sound at the laryngeal level. There are various theories to account for it, but none is based on sufficient evidence to state with certainty just how phonation occurs. The speech pathologist should be acquainted with the most significant theories of phonation because they provide a framework against which observation of phonatory problems in retardates may be described. Discussions of these theories are found in most basic textbooks on speech pathology, so the matter will not be discussed here.

Developmental changes of laryngeal structures occur with age, and although not as observable as some other maturational changes, they are basic to understanding phonatory problems. The length of the vocal folds changes from 3 mm at 3 days to 5.5 mm at 12 months of age. In adult males, the length is between 17 and 23 mm and in adult females it is from 12 to 17 mm. Growth of the arytenoid cartilage stabilizes at about 1 year of age, the same time at which most children learn their first word. If growth of the vocal folds is delayed along with other physical growth, voice-quality differences may result.

The responsibility of the speech pathologist is primarily one of recognition of the acoustic parameters of voice that are indicative of laryngeal dysfunction or the phonatory process. In infancy, stridor in cry is a clue that laryngeal pathology may be present. Later, the speech pathologist should be alert to harshness in the voice, which frequently has its origin in too much tension of the muscles of the neck and throat as well as the larynx. Tenseness is observable during speech and also is palpable by placing the fingers on either side of the larynx. This also may be associated with quality and pitch problems.

It has been said frequently that there is a typical voice quality characteristic of the mentally retarded. This quality has been characterized as: husky, hoarse, low-pitched, monotonous, gurgling, and of an inconsistent intensity not appropriate to content. Experimental research has not demonstrated conclusively that there is a typical voice quality used by the retarded, but clinicians do consistently report voice deviations among the mentally retarded. It may be safe to say that such deviations might be expected with more frequency among the retarded than among the nonretarded. Perhaps the most consistently reported voice characteristic is that of the mongoloid, who very frequently presents a clinical picture of a husky, somewhat flat, hoarse voice quality, with faulty phrasing.

There is some evidence from the work of Michel and Carney (70) and Hollien and Copeland (36) that listeners may perceive lower pitch in the presence of harshness when that pitch is not present by objective analysis. These investigators found that the fundamental frequency of the mongoloid's voice approximated the norms for "normal" speakers of comparable age levels. Although the speech samples used in the norms and the speech samples of the mongoloid children were not the same, the information from these studies suggests that the previous descriptions of the mongoloid voice as being low pitched and harsh is open to question.

Breathiness was discussed in the section on respiration, but the condition also may have its origin in improper movement of the vocal folds, which allows air to escape through the glottis without being controlled for speech production. Breathiness frequently is associated with inadequate loudness. Instrumentation for analysis of breathiness in the voice has found little clinical use and the speech pathologist is again dependent upon his ability to hear the escape of air and to judge, with some degree of consistency, when this occurs.

Hoarseness combines the characteristics used to describe harshness and breathiness, and often is found to be of transient quality associated with colds and upper-respiratory infections. However, it also may be chronic and usually is associated with laryngeal pathology. Edema of vocal folds, carcinoma of the larynx, contact ulcers, vocal nodules, polyps, vocal abuse, excessive loud talking, and use of improper pitch level all have been mentioned as causes of hoarseness.

Many of the retarded are mouth breathers and tongue thrusters—perhaps giving rise to some oral structural deviations and interference with speech, and also related to respiration and nasal cleanliness. There is considerable recurring nasal congestion among the retarded, which contributes to various voice problems.

In all of the problems of phonation, the speech pathologist is largely dependent upon accurate, carefully collected case-history information on the development and duration of the condition. This should be supplied to the otolaryngologist, and careful medical examination should help determine whether these voice characteristics exist on the basis of organic factors or reflect habitual use of patterns of phonation that may be expected to yield to training.

Resonation

Many speech pathologists prefer to discuss resonation and articulation as the same process. However, in the case of the mentally retarded child, there seems to be some justification for discussing them separately. It should be remembered, though, that the two are very closely associated and modifications in either may affect the other. Resonance refers to the vibratory response of the air-filled cavities (hypopharynx, oral pharynx, epipharynx, oral, sinus, and nasal cavities) to a frequency imposed upon it. These air-filled cavities selectively modify the laryngeal tone, resulting in distinctive quality characteristics.

The size and shape of these resonating cavities change with advancing age and, as in other growth processes, the changes may be delayed in the mentally retarded child. The shape of the oral pharynx and epipharynx is modified primarily by the presence of pharyngeal tonsils and adenoids or by some structural defect such as cleft palate or paralysis. If any of these structures is chronically infected or enlarged, it may alter the natural quality of the individual's voice. If adenoids are enlarged to the extent that the nasal consonants cannot be amplified in the nasal cavity, speech will be distorted. Articulation of *m, n,* and ŋ will be affected. This also may occur with chronic rhinitis or allergy.

It already has been pointed out that palatal deviations are common among mentally retarded children. A short soft palate with resulting inadequate palato-pharyngeal closure frequently causes too much nasal resonance or hypernasality. It often is associated with a bifid uvula and a submucous cleft of the hard or soft palate. The same problem may be caused by sluggish movement of the soft palate or movements that are poorly timed in relation to the production of the laryngeal tone. The speech pathologist who works with a mentally retarded population should be very alert to this problem because it affects articulation as well as resonance.

According to Critchley (15) the loudness, pitch, and quality of children's voices commonly reach the standards of social acceptability at about $4\frac{1}{2}$ years of age; one would expect this to be delayed in mentally retarded children.

Articulation

Articulation problems are almost universally recognized as the most prevalent of all speech disorders and this certainly holds true in the mentally retarded. Powers (74) has defined articulation as the production of speech sounds by the stopping or constricting of the vocalized or nonvocalized breath stream by movements of the lips, tongue, velum, or pharynx. She states that "disorders of articulation are faulty placement, timing, direction, pressure, speed, or integration of these movements, resulting in absent or incorrect speech sounds." In analyzing the articulation problems of the mentally retarded child, careful observation frequently will reveal more than one of these faults in the articulatory process.

By far the most typical articulation pattern presented by the mentally retarded child is one of immaturity. If the sounds being misarticulated are compared with the developmental norms of Templin (87), one usually finds that the child is using sounds consistent with or below his mental age rather than his chronological age.

Another aspect of the usual articulation pattern of retarded children is found in the type of error. Milisen (71) has suggested that if a child makes mostly errors of omitting sounds, he is more retarded in articulation than the child who uses substitutions. Likewise, the child who uses substitutions is more retarded in articulation than the child who distorts sounds. It has been observed clinically that retarded children make far more errors of omission than substitution or distortion. In fact, it is not unusual for the retarded child to articulate words by producing only the initial consonant and the vowel that follows. Children of normal intelligence often do this at young age levels. Awareness of the developmental aspects of articulation will assist the speech pathologist in assessing the developmental level of the retarded child's articulation.

Numerous articulation tests have been developed over the years and most of them will be useful to the speech pathologist evaluating the articulation of the retarded child. Only a few of the specific tests will be described here. The Arizona Articulation Test developed by Barker and England (8) utilizes pictures as the stimulus material for eliciting responses from the child, and the child's performance is reported as an articulation proficiency score. This score is computed by assigning to each sound weighted values derived from the study of frequency of occurrence of American speech sounds reported by French, Carter, and Koenig (23). This provides a precise measure that is useful in assessing progress as well as evaluating the status of articulation skill at any given time. If the child does not name the pictures, the test may be administered by getting the child to repeat the words after the examiner.

The Templin Darley Diagnostic Articulation Test (88) also has been widely used. This test consists of 176 items that test all vowels and diphthongs once, every consonant once in each position in which it occurs, and each of the more frequently occurring consonant blends. Frequently, the mentally retarded child will not attend to the task long enough to complete this test in one session. Use of the 50 screening items of this test will provide an indication of the child's articulation skills that can be completed in one session.

Whatever test of articulation the speech pathologist uses, the results should be carefully analyzed. Relationships between articulation errors and deviations in function of the articulators should be noted. More discussion of these relationships will appear in the chapter on management of speech and language problems, but a few things should be stated here. The consonants requiring the most intraoral breath pressure are the affricates, fricatives, and plosives—in that order. Also, Black (10) has shown that voiceless consonant sounds require more pressure than their voiced cognates. Since the affricates and fricatives are later-developing consonant sounds, many speech pathologists fail to recognize errors on these sounds as an indication of poor palato-pharyngeal closure. There are several clues that are helpful in this regard. Usually, there is some nasal emission of air during attempted production of the sibilant sounds, and possibly on most consonant sounds—including plosives if the inadequacy is great. The voice quality may be hypernasal, and the alae of the nose may constrict during consonant production. The child may substitute a glottal stop for the high-pressure consonant sounds, or he may substitute an aspirated *h* for them.

If the mentally retarded child is also hard of hearing, this may be indicated by errors on consonant sounds that have poor visibility while those that are easily identified visually are produced more accurately. If the hearing loss relates only to sounds of high frequency, articulation errors may occur only on sounds such as s, $\int$, or f.

Mention was made in an earlier chapter that malocclusion often is present in retarded children. Open bite as one type of malocclusion frequently is associated with a tongue-thrust pattern of swallow. Both of these defects appear to be related to distorted production of s, z, $\int$, t, $ʒ$, and $dʒ$ consonants. Fletcher *et al.* (21) report a decreasing incidence of these problems with age, so it does not seem unusual to find an increased incidence in the mentally retarded population.

Articulation is affected by other maturational changes in oral structures. In the early months and years, the tongue is very close to the palate. It gradually assumes a lower position that usually is achieved by 3 years of age. If these changes are delayed in the retarded child, as they often are, the result may be immature articulation of sounds. Many retarded children have been observed to articulate the tongue tip sounds with the midportion of the tongue. They also demonstrate an inability to lift the tongue tip without pushing it upward with the mandible. Even if the sounds are intelligible to the listener, these immature patterns of function should be noted.

Articulation, then, is a complicated process that may be deviant in many ways in retarded as well as in non-retarded children. Certainly, it is not enough to say the retarded child has an articulation problem. Further analysis needs to be made and relationships between the articulation errors and impairment of functions of speech articulators observed, if such are present. The nature of the errors needs to be described and related to physical structures. If modification of faulty structures is possible, appropriate steps should be taken. Efficient articulation skills are essential for the retarded child if he is to communicate effectively with others.

Symbolization

In order to utilize meaningfully the basic processes discussed thus far, an individual must be capable of understanding and using the linguistic code of his family and his community. In other words, symbolization is the ability to understand and formulate the symbolic forms of language. It involves learning the rules of the language and developing patterns of applying those rules, along with understanding the rules and symbols as they are used by others. It is convenient to discuss the comprehension aspects of symbolization as separate from the expressive aspects even though it is more difficult to view them separately in reality.

Development of tests to measure the comprehension of language has been slow to occur. Bangs (7) has developed a battery for this purpose by selecting subtests from the Revised Stanford-Binet Intelligence Scale, Forms L and M, (89), and the Gesell Developmental Scale (27). Although this battery gives useful information, it frequently presents complications when these tests also are being used to assess the intellectual functioning of the same child. Sections of the Illinois Test of Psycho-Linguistic

Abilities (50) deal with comprehension of language. Even though this test is still in an experimental edition, some helpful information is available from the sections on auditory decoding and auditory association. Many parents report that a child understands everything said to him. Performance on decoding helps establish the level at which the child understands language. Errors in auditory association may show a pattern that can be improved.

Another measure of comprehension of language was developed at the University of Oregon Medical School and is known as the Manual for Evaluation of Speech, Hearing, and Language (62). Its usefulness has been limited by the fact that it is an assembly of items developed clinically, and others reported in the literature, and has not been adequately standardized. Nevertheless, measures of comprehension, using this test as a guide, have shown very close agreement with mental age levels established through Stanford-Binet (89) and the Wechsler Intelligence Scale for Children (90). A project is currently underway that will standardize a refined version of this manual by using a large number of children in the Portland, Oregon area.

Recognition vocabulary measures also have been used as methods of estimating a child's ability to comprehend language. Several good ones are available. The Ammons Full Range Picture Vocabularly Test (1) presents a sample of 85 words. The subject responds by pointing to the picture that shows the meaning of the word given by the examiner. The age level at which 50 percent of a representative population would fail the word determines the point level for each word. The subject's score (total of correct responses) can be converted to a mental age.

The Peabody Picture Vocabulary Test (18) is somewhat similar. It consists of 150 words arranged in order of increasing difficulty. Instructions for establishing a basal level and a ceiling level are given in the examiner's manual. The subject chooses one of four pictures that best represents the word named by the examiner. His score is the number of correct responses and may be converted to a mental age, a standard score, IQ, or a percentile. Standardization was done using more than 4,000 subjects, but the test's agreement with mental age established through the use of Stanford-Binet or WISC intelligence tests has shown some variability. This likely is because of the fact that some children will be strong or weak in vocabulary skill, and vary in other skills measured by intelligence tests. However, the test is a useful one if it is part of a battery of tests or is used as a screening device.

Most measurements of expressive language skills also have utilized vocabulary measures. The age of first-word usage generally has been considered a significant development landmark. It may serve as a gross indicator of retardation, but because of the tremendous variability in reporting and time of first-word occurrence in normal children, it should be used with caution. Generally speaking, most children use their first word around their first birthday. Vocabulary gradually increases with age—as shown by word counts of the number of different words used, reported by Smith (83). Beyond the age of 2 years, the child uses so many different words that the measure is somewhat cumbersome as a clinical evaluation technique. There is a rapid increase from about 22 words at 18 months to 272 words at 24 months. Many retarded children do not show this rapid increase in vocabulary usage until much later than 2 years, and often show even a more gradual increase.

Many speech pathologists agree that the most reliable measure of verbal expression is the mean length of response. This test was developed by McCarthy (63), and considerable research is reported concerning it. One simply records fifty responses of a child who may be encouraged to talk about pictures, toys, or talk with his mother about a topic of their choice. The number of words used in each response is totaled according to simple rules stated by McCarthy (63). Then all responses are totaled and the mean number of words is determined by dividing this total by 50, the number of responses. A time-saving but less reliable measure is the mean of the five longest responses used by the child. Means and standard deviations for the length of response measures at yearly age levels are reported by Johnson, Darley, and Spriestersbach (43). A word of caution is necessary concerning mean length of response as a measure of expressive speech of the retarded child. It is not uncommon to find a retarded child who perseverates so extensively that his mean length of response will be impressive, yet the responses are largely irrelevant. Many retardates also learn to use a surprising number of fairly complex, seemingly appropriate responses, such as "How do you do, Mr. X. I hope you are well today." Eventually it is discovered that this repertoire is limited and must serve for many inappropriate occasions. Mean length of response again is a good measure, but it may be misleading.

Numerous other measures of verbal expression have

been proposed, but they involve so much computation that they have found little place in the clinical evaluation of language skills of children, retarded or nonretarded. The verbal encoding section of the Illinois Test of Psycho-Linguistic Abilities (50) holds some promise, but it has consistently shown depression in relation to skills in other areas. It is possible that the revision of this test will modify this discrepancy.

The Michigan Picture Language Inventory (55) contains a section that develops a language structure expression score. After the examiner has described the picture cards to the child, the child is asked to describe them for the examiner. The total of correct responses according to the four function classes of words developed by Fries (24) represents the verbal usage score. These scores are of increasing magnitude at successive age levels.

One other analysis of verbal expression that should be mentioned is the verbal analysis of Skinner (82). He divides expressive language into five types: (1) tact, (2) mand, (3) echoic, (4) interverbal, and (5) autoclitic. Little research is yet available regarding the developmental sequence of these types of responses. Eventually, research employing this technique may yield worthwhile developmental information. In the meantime, it is useful for describing types of verbal responses.

Instruments designed specifically for assessing the speech and language problems of the mentally retarded are not plentiful, but a few have been developed and are promising. One of them was developed by Lassers and Low (53). A major part of this project consisted of developing a test battery for the assessment of communicative attributes in the mentally retarded. This battery appears to hold considerable promise for the diagnostician working with the mentally retarded. Another very promising diagnostic tool for the mentally retarded is one of the procedures used in the Parsons Project (78). The Parsons Language Sample was designed specifically as a means of obtaining and describing language output of mentally retarded children. It provided a useful means of quantifying language in the Parsons Project, and the method of eliciting speech has been found useful in clinical evaluations of retarded children.

Most references cited thus far include good discussions of the development of speech and language, but they tend to neglect the early years from birth to age 3 years. The Oregon Manual (62), the Mecham Scale (68), and the Crabtree Scale (14), do include these lower age levels. Table 7 presents brief descriptions of language skills based on a number of the above-mentioned references. It is useful with children from birth through age 6 years. The obvious limitation of this guide involves the lack of standardized method of making observations regarding the language skills described.

Audition

The process of audition is one that is highly unobservable and, therefore, it is difficult to describe. Various attempts to determine the maturational aspects of audition and to define it have been made. For example, Critchley (15) states the hearing requirements for speech

T A B L E 7. PATTERN OF NORMAL LANGUAGE DEVELOPMENT

Age (mo.)	Vocalization	Response to vocal sound
1	Crying, whimpering, produces all vowels and consonants *k,g,h*. Sighs, grunts, explosives.	
2 & 3	Pitch of crying slightly higher. More noncrying vocalizing. Different kind of crying for pain, hunger, etc. Some repetitive vocalizing, *gagaga*, etc. Adds consonant ŋ.	Sometimes smiles or is soothed by pleasant adult voice. Responds to adult cooing, etc., by repeating own formerly practiced sounds. Sometimes stops vocalizing when adult enters in. May cry in response to angry voice; coo, sigh, gurgle in response to pleasant voice.
4	More babbling and vocal play, repetitive vocalizing—mostly when child is alone. Smiles, laughs, gurgles, coos when comfortable.	Imitative response to speech decreases and doesn't reappear until about ninth month. Indiscriminate interruption of babbling causes child to stop vocalizing.
5	Increase of above. Occasionally responds to parental babbling if done softly and not interrupting child's vocal play.	Responds to voices by turning eye and head. Automatic response to friendly and angry tone. Vocalizes displeasure—losing toy, etc.
6	More repetitive babbling, with marked rhythm. Increase in intensity from whisper. More noncrying sounds. Nasal tone begins to be heard. Some tongue-tip activity begins.	Response to friendly or angry tone not automatic, but depends on other aspects of the situation: gestures, physical contact, etc.
7	More variety. Dissyllables. Same sounds repeated several days. Uses *m,n,b,p,d,t* in babbling.	Mostly rejects demands for imitation of sounds. Responds to gestures accompanied by voice.
8	Begins to imitate own vocal play—"mama," "dada," "bye bye," but not in response to adults. Babbling shows pitch and inflection change. Increased tongue-tip activity.	Calls for attention. Combines babbling with gestures. Perseverates in imitating hand clapping, etc., accompanied by voice.

T A B L E 7. *(Continued)*

Age (mo.)	Vocalization	Response to vocal sound
9	More variety in crying and babbling, more back vowels used. Higher pitch and more pitch variation. Cries to get attention. More vocalizing is babbling rather than crying.	Retreats from strangers and mostly from other children by crying. Holds out arms to be picked up if adult extends arms. Not much imitative response to accompanying vocalization.
10	Makes effort to imitate others. Can imitate if adults use same sounds, as in child's vocal play. May use one word correctly.	Begins to comprehend "no no," "dada," etc. Will respond to words, "patty-cake," "bye bye," with gestures.
11	Can imitate correct number of syllables and sounds heard in adult vocal stimulation. Imitates some new sounds not previously used.	Shows interest in isolated words associated with objects or activities important to the child. Will imitate two tones sung by an adult.
12	Some echolalia if sounds introduced unobtrusively by adults. Accompanies vocalization with gestures. May acquire first true word (s). Much interest in isolated words connected with own needs and activities.	Sometimes will imitate dogs, clocks, cows, etc., or adult exclamations. Imitates adult words with initial sound(s). "Pup" = p or p_A. Often imitates dissyllabic words.

Age (yr.)	Expressive speech	Comprehension of speech
1–2	Uses 1 to 3 words at 12 mo., 10 to 15 at 15 mo., 15 to 20 at 18 mo., about 100–200 by 2 yr. Knows names of most objects he uses. Names few people, uses verbs but not correctly with subjects. Jargon and echolalia. Names 1–3 pictures.	Begins to relate symbol and object meaning. Adjusts to comments. Inhibits on command. Responds correctly to "give me that," "sit down," "stand up" with gestures. Puts watch to ear on command. Understands simple questions. Recognizes 120–275 words.
2–3	Vocabulary increases to 300–500 words. Says "where kitty?," "ball all gone," "want cookie,"	Rapid increase in comprehension vocabulary to 400 at 2½, 800 at 3. Responds to commands using

T A B L E 7. *(Continued)*

Age (yr.)	Expressive speech	Comprehension of speech
	"go bye bye car." Jargon mostly gone. Vocalizing increases. Has fluency trouble. Speech not adequate for communication needs.	"on," "under," "up," "down," "over there," "by," "run," "walk," "jump up," "throw," "run fast," "be quiet," and commands containing two related actions.
3–4	Uses 600–1000 words, becomes conscious of speech. 3–4 words per speech response. Personal pronouns, some adjectives, adverbs, and prepositions appear. Mostly simple sentences, but some complex. Speech more useful.	Understands up to 1500 words by age 4. Recognizes plurals, sex difference, pronouns, adjectives. Comprehends complex and compound sentences. Answers simple questions.
4–5	Increase in vocabulary to 1000–1600 words. More 3–4 syllable words. More adjectives, adverbs, prepositions, and conjunctions. Articles appear. Sentences of 4, 5, 6 words, syntax quite good. Uses plurals. Fluency improves. Proper nouns decrease, pronouns increase.	Comprehends 1500–2000 words. Carries out more complex commands, with 2–3 actions. Understands dependent clause, "if," "because," "when," "why."
5–6	Increase in vocabulary to 1500–2100 words. Complete 5–6-word sentences, compound, complex, with some dependent clauses. Syntax near normal. Quite fluent. More multisyllable words.	Understands vocabulary of 2500–2800 words. Responds correctly to more complicated sentences but is still confused at times by involved sentences.

Age (yr.)	Articulation	General intelligibility
1–2	Uses all vowels and consonants *m,b,p,k,g,w,h,n,t,d.* Omits most final consonants, some initial. Substitutes consonants above for more difficult. Much unin-	Words used may be no more than 25 percent intelligible to unfamiliar listener. Jargon near 18 mo. almost 100 percent unintelligible. Improvement noticeable

T A B L E 7. *(Continued)*

Age (yr.)	Articulation	General intelligibility
	telligible jargon around 18 mo. Good inflection, rate.	between 21 and 24 months.
2–3	Continues all sounds above with vowels but use is inconsistent. Tries many new sounds, but poor mastery. Much substitution. Omission of final consonants. Articulation lags behind vocabulary.	Words about 65 percent intelligible by 2 years; 70–80 percent intelligible in context by 3. Many individual sounds faulty but total context generally understood. Some incomprehensibility because of faulty sentence structure.
3–4	Masters p,b,t,d,k,g, and tries many others including f,v,θ,δ, s, z, and consonant combinations tr,bl,pr,gr,dr, but r and l may be faulty so substitutes w or omits. Speech almost intelligible. Uses θ,δ inconsistently.	Speech usually 90–100 percent intelligible in context. Individual sounds still faulty and some trouble with sentence structure.
4–5	Masters f and v and many consonant combinations. Should be little omission of initial and final consonants. Fewer substitutes but may be some. May distort r,l,s,z, $\int$, $t\int$, d_3,θ,δ. No trouble with multisyllable words.	Speech is intelligible in context even though some sounds are still faulty.
5–6	Masters r,l,θ,δ, and such blends as tl,gr,bl,br,pr, etc. May still have some trouble with blends such as $\int r,sk,st,\theta r$. May still distort s,z, $\int,t\int$, d_3. May not master these sounds until age 7½.	Good.

SOURCE: H. Lillywhite. "Doctor's Manual of Speech Disorders." *Journal of the American Medical Association,* Vol. 167, June, 1958. Pp. 850–851.

as "brain stem startle reflexes, cortical representation of hearing, development of association areas, and feedback mechanisms." Lloyd and Frisina (59) state that the auditory system is important for "its handling of auditory symbols mechanically, chemically, and electrically, as well as for the subsequent transmission of coded neural impulses to the areas of the brain important for speech and language. Important CNS processes include those such as perception, concept development, and ideation." On the other hand, Kendall (48) identifies "audition" as "something that recognizes, discriminates, identifies, interprets sound and selects from all the stimuli that engage the ear particular arrangements and patternings that carry meaning, can be organized, classified and related to past experience."

Encompassed in all these definitions of audition are the requirements that the process involves awareness of sound, recognition of sound, and interpretation of sound. In evaluating the mentally retarded child's abilities in audition, it is important to remember that evidence indicating awareness of sound is not assurance that he can recognize and interpret that sound for purposes of language learning. However, methods of evaluating recognition and interpretation abilities are quite limited at this time and the audiologist often must be content with evidence that the mentally retarded child is aware of sounds at loudness levels consistent with ability to learn language. Many children who are retarded will respond to standard methods of testing hearing. A child can be instructed to raise his hand when the tone comes on and to lower his hand when the tone goes away. Most children who have achieved a mental age of around 3 years will respond to this standard method of testing hearing with pure-tone audiometry.

Below the mental age of approximately 3 years, techniques of testing used with normal young children are appropriate. Some children can respond to the presence of a sound, usually a pure tone, by the usual play audiometry techniques in which they put a peg in a board, a marble in a jar, one block on top of another, etc., when they hear the stimulus. This type of testing usually requires two trained examiners, one with the child and one with the equipment. Verbal instructions to the child frequently confuse responses more than clarifying them. Often, it seems best simply to condition the child to put a peg in the board when the tone comes on by doing it for him at first, then assisting him, and finally it is necessary to gradually withdraw the examiner's assistance. Once a response pattern has been established, it is important to work as rapidly as possible so that the child maintains attention to the task. The examiner with the child needs to encourage the child and help maintain the response by showing approval.

If the mentally retarded child is not able to learn a response pattern and use it consistently, it is possible to gain some assessment of awareness of sound by using calibrated noisemakers and observing reactions to them. Most children who have achieved a mental age of 8 months will localize sounds effectively. Accurate localization of sounds presented above and below the ear level, as well as level with it, show recognition of the position of the sound and indicate more adequate development of audition than a response that searches for the sound. Many children at the 8-month level of mental development will respond to "cry sounds" and music at lower loudness levels than they will respond to pure tones.

The majority of retarded children can be tested with

the standard methods described above if the appropriate ones for their mental development are chosen. However, around 10 to 15 percent will not respond to such attempts to assess hearing. For this group, the examiner must rely on other procedures. Although special tests such as EEG and GSR have been used, the results are not so reliable with retarded children as with other groups. In addition, results of studies to date indicate the value of GSR techniques in research, but are inconclusive with respect to testing retarded children. The use of EEG audiometric techniques is limited and still considered in the investigative stages. These two techniques are of value, but at the present time are more likely to be used in large centers than by the average clinician.

Another technique which has come to be known as Operant Conditioning Audiometry (OCA) holds more promise for providing a means of testing individuals who do not respond adequately to standard audiometric techniques. The specific routines developed in this method of testing hearing vary for each examiner and often for each individual being tested. Several conditioning routines and a wide variety of reinforcing techniques are useful, but none of these has been found to be effective with all individuals. The reader is referred to the excellent conference report *Audiologic Assessment of the Mentally Retarded* by Lloyd and Frisina (59) for more complete discussion of this topic.

Successful testing for speech reception thresholds is possible with most of the retarded children. Some of them will be able to respond by repeating the word in the traditional manner. Others will be able to point to the picture and others will respond by picking up the appropriate toy. Ryan and Stewart (77) have reported successful testing using animal noises and having the child touch the correct picture associated with the noise. Speech reception thresholds have been obtained on some children who did not respond adequately to pure-tone threshold testing.

It is evident that testing of audition among the mentally retarded requires more time than for normal individuals and it may require different methods of testing that utilize more tangible rewards for responses. It is entirely possible that a hearing loss of a given degree may affect the retarded child's ability to acquire language to a greater extent than the same hearing loss would affect a nonretarded individual. It is extremely important to determine hearing levels at the earliest age level possible and to make every effort to provide corrective measures when feasible. Any well-trained audiologist experienced with nonretarded children may expect to modify his routines of testing considerably for the retarded child. These modifications may result from experience or from following the experiences of others who have worked with retarded children.

Summary

In summary, it may be said that the speech pathologist evaluating mentally retarded children should expect many of the same kinds of speech, language, and hearing problems that are found in the nonretarded population. Such factors as structural malformations, specific neurological deficiencies, environmental, social, and emotional problems will influence speech, language, and hearing development among the retarded. It should be noted, however, that perhaps these factors may have greater impact on the mentally retarded than the nonretarded, as the retarded child is likely to be more vulnerable to anything that adversely influences development.

It must be pointed out also that there are as wide variations among the speech, language, and hearing abilities of the retarded as among the nonretarded; that is, there will be some with rather marked retardation who are more verbal than would be expected, and have fewer speech disorders, especially articulatory; and there are some with mild retardation who present, frequently for unknown reasons, markedly deficient speech and language. Although there is likely to be a higher proportion of speech, language, and hearing problems among children at all levels of retardation, it should be remembered that as Schlanger and Gottsleben (80) state:

Mental retardation is not an entity but a symptom complex as it is caused not only by pathology of the physical system, especially the central nervous system, but also by defects in the psychological and sociological spheres. One should not diagnose speech problems as being *caused* by mental retardation. An awareness of this by speech clinicians invites a more searching investigation into speech problems.

The task of the speech and language diagnostician with the mentally retarded, then, obviously is a rather broad one—demanding considerable understanding of the total process of normal speech and language development and the ability to recognize delay aspects and to differentiate them from other types of deviations. It will be as necessary in the diagnosis of communication disorders to do a differential diagnosis as it was in the total diagnostic process of establishing mental retardation.

Supplemental references

Brose, David C. "The Mongoloid Voice." Unpublished paper, University of Oregon, 1966.

de Hirsch, Katrina. "Studies in Tachyphemia: IV. Diagnosis of Developmental Language Disorders." *Logos,* Vol. 4, No. 1, 1961. Pp. 3–9.

Falck, F. J., and V. T. Falck. "Disorders of Neurological Integrative Mechanisms—A Rationale for the Expansion of Our Professional Scope." *ASHA,* Vol. 4, No. 12, December, 1962. Pp. 439–440.

Hardy, W. G. "On Language Disorders in Young Children: A Reorganization of Thinking." *Journal of Speech and Hearing Disorders,* Vol. 30, No. 1, 1965. Pp. 3–17.

Lloyd, L. L., M. J. Reed, and D. L. McManis. "The Effect of Response Mode on the SRT's Obtained from Retarded Children." *Journal of Auditory Research,* Vol. 7, No. 3, 1967. Pp. 219–222.

McIntire, Matilda, J. Wiley, and W. Wolski. "Central Language Disorders as Seen in a Mental Retardation Evaluation Clinic." *Lancet,* Vol. 86, No. 7, 1966. Pp. 374–378.

Peins, Maryann. "Mental Retardation: A Selected Bibliography of Speech, Hearing, and Language Problems." *ASHA,* Vol. 4, No. 2, 1962. Pp. 38–40.

Rochford, G., and M. Williams. "The Measurement of Language Disorders." *Speech Pathology and Therapy,* Vol. 7, No. 1, 1964. Pp. 3–21.

Schlanger, B. B., and G. I. Galanowsky. "Auditory Discrimination Tasks Performed by Mentally Retarded and Normal Children." *Journal of Speech and Hearing Research,* Vol. 9, No. 3, September, 1966. Pp. 434–440.

Spradlin, J. E. "Language and Communication of Mental Defectives." In Ellis, N. R., ed., *Handbook of Mental Deficiency.* New York, McGraw-Hill, 1963. Pp. 512–555.

Wood, Nancy E. *Language Disorders in Children.* Chicago, National Society for Crippled Children and Adults, 1959. Pp. 1–21.

CHAPTER 7

Management of communication disorders

Actual therapy procedures for the communication problems of the mentally retarded may be no more complicated than for most of the other severe disorders. That is, the improvement of communication behavior may not present highly unusual problems, especially from the standpoint of speech; however, the aspects of prognosis, justification for therapy, and progress assume more than ordinary importance.

These aspects are not peculiar to the problem of mental retardation, as the clinician dealing with any type of problem must make decisions as to whether a particular patient justifies therapy and, if so, how much, what kind, and for how long. In most other instances, however, there are rather clear-cut factors that will give a fairly accurate prognosis and will suggest a therapy plan, if one is to be instigated.

In mental retardation the problem is complicated by the fact that because mental age and communication abilities relate very directly to each other, the clinician may be tempted to rely on mental age as an adequate prognostic indicator with respect to speech and language therapy. It is true that mental age is perhaps the best guide, but the factors of social age, over-all delayed development, the likelihood of accompanying emotional disturbances, perhaps a severely restricted experience, lack of motivation, and the child's inability to see cause-and-effect relationships all conspire to complicate the question of prognosis, justification, and measurement of progress of speech and language therapy.

In addition, the clinician is faced with a widespread, long-standing attitude among speech specialists that therapy for the mentally retarded generally is not worthwhile because the results are too minimal to justify the expenditure of time, personnel, and money. Many speech and hearing clinics still exclude from therapy children known to be retarded, and many school systems with special classes for the retarded do not offer speech therapy for children in such classes.

Such an attitude may be reasonable in many cases, yet its generalized acceptance certainly shows an inflexibility that does not do justice to the profession. As Matthews (67) has pointed out, "There is little research data to guide us in the acceptance or rejection of the advisability of attempting speech therapy with the severely retarded."

There is no simple answer to the question as to whether to institute or continue therapy; the question can be answered only on the basis of the individual case as presented with all of its ramifications.

Perhaps, however, it is safe to generalize to the extent that the less complicated the case—from the standpoint of other anomalies and negative environmental factors—the better the mentally retarded child will respond to speech and language therapy. Those at the upper end of the educable group offer the best prognosis; those at the lower end, the least. In the trainable group there is still less favorable prognosis and less justification for extensive therapy as the intelligence level goes down. Very few specialists would argue that extensive speech and language training for the custodial group can be justified. However, specific communication needs for individuals at all levels of retardation must be considered and goals of therapy established in accordance with these needs.

The speech clinician must rely upon an adequate individualized diagnosis of the over-all retardation as well as a differential diagnosis of the communication problem. To adopt a blanket policy of either offering or not offering speech and language therapy to the mentally retarded is a shortsighted and inappropriate approach to the problem. Such factors as case load, the time available, and the policy of the institution or school system will demand that the speech clinician establish some priorities for offering speech services. It becomes necessary, then, for the speech clinician to develop a realistic policy regarding the acceptance or rejection of individuals for speech and language therapy and he should follow the policy consistently in making decisions about individual clients.

One fact that quickly becomes clear to the clinician working with the mentally retarded is that the parents of the retarded, as well as many professionals, have the mistaken notion that "if the child could just talk better, he would be all right." On the basis of this "if" they often demand therapy when it is not indicated or is impossible to provide, and they place a great deal of pressure on the speech clinician for speech and language training. The assumption that if the child had adequate speech he would be "all right" is, of course, correct in most cases; but the fact that he does not have adequate speech rarely is because of lack of therapy. It is much more complex than this, and the speech clinician should be prepared to explain the many factors in retardation that cause communication disorders. Discussion of the nature of speech and language skills expected at the mental age of a given child often will help parents understand that the problem involves more than "not talking."

Still another factor that bears upon this problem is that of mental age in relation to chronological age. One of the most frequent errors made by parents of the retarded, and sometimes by professionals working with them, is the attempt to evaluate the child in terms of chronological age and to try to hold him to a chronological age standard in speech and language. The result has been that many retarded children have been pushed beyond their capacity to the point that severely negative attitudes toward better speech and language are created.

A very important aspect of this problem, also, is the

fact that a retarded child's speech and language rarely are commensurate with his mental age, let alone his chronological age. Parents and most professionals outside of the field of speech do not recognize this fact, but there is much clinical evidence that the speech and language levels almost always will be somewhat below the mental age of the retarded child. The degree of difference between mental age and speech and language age will depend primarily on the extent of retardation, but also will be subject to many other factors such as speech and language environment and other retarding aspects.

In the Lillywhite study (58) previously mentioned, 80 percent of the children studied were retarded below their mental age in all language areas. The communication profiles of these retarded children demonstrate the typical gap between speech and language levels and mental age. It is this gap between mental age and levels of speech and language abilities that gives the speech clinician a basis for justifying speech and language training. Potentially, each child should be able to use speech and language that is commensurate with his mental age. Accompanying retardation factors, however, probably account for the fact that he usually fails to do so. In the cases without additional complicating factors, or when these factors can be modified, the speech clinician may find quite a favorable prognosis—certainly one can justify offering therapy directed at developing the child's communication abilities until they are consistent with his mental age.

Another consideration with respect to mental age and communication proficiency is that the clinician must avoid the temptation to try to push the child beyond his capabilities. The mental age will be the upper limit and only a few will reach that level. In most cases, all concerned must settle for less than "normal" and frequently for less than "adequate" communication skills. The best that can be hoped for in many cases will be some increase in the child's ability to function somewhat more adequately as a social being, that is, to communicate better than he has been able to communicate, although he may still do so with a great many errors and with a minimal vocabulary.

Perhaps it will be difficult in a majority of instances to justify intensive, long-term work on articulation deviations that do not seriously interfere with the child's communication. An individual can make many speech errors and still communicate fairly well. Perhaps this is the best that can be achieved with many of the mentally retarded. On the other hand, retardates suffer enough handicaps without the additional one of speech and language errors. For this reason, every effort should be made to give them the best speech and language of which they are capable. The speech clinician should attempt to establish the limits of capability, and then work within them.

Although both language and speech frequently deviate together, it is possible that one process is adequate while the other is inadequate. The work of Penfield and Roberts (73) indicates that there may be very good evidence that the brain centers for speech and language are quite separate, one from the other. This view is in agreement with that of many neurologists.

It is important that the speech clinician called upon to

diagnose and to help improve the communication problems of the mentally retarded develop some awareness of the relationships between language and speech if the two are considered separate entities. It follows, then, that if the child's communication problem is primarily one of basic language deficiency, that is, a lack of structural framework for the formulation of symbolic concepts, then the speech clinician's beginning point is obvious. The first job would be to establish a vocabulary and language framework upon which the child can develop useful speech. Without a basic language of some consistency, adequate speech will not develop.

General principles of therapy

There are several general principles that may serve as guidelines in developing programs of speech and language therapy for mentally retarded individuals. They could be stated in a number of different ways, but need to embody the following concepts.

1. Management procedures should be based on adequate differential diagnosis of the communication deficiencies of the individual child.

2. Communication therapy should begin at the maximum level the child has reached in comprehension of verbal symbols, language concepts, sentence structure, articulation ability, intelligibility, and expression.

3. Establishment of a minimal basic language structure should precede intensive work on the refinement of speech —such as in articulation and intelligibility.

4. Generally, a developmental order of language and speech should be followed—but with the realization that every child need not necessarily pass through such stages as babbling and jargon.

5. If possible, a social and psychological environment that will be highly stimulating and motivating for language development should be established.

6. The speech clinician will need to rely primarily on group social experiential situations rather than individual drill-type sessions for the development of all aspects of speech and language. Much repetition of familiar communication experiences will be necessary.

7. The speech clinician will need to make extensive use of the home, the classroom, and other people and situations in the child's environment in order to provide concrete, vivid experiences linked with verbalization of the experiences and experiential concepts.

8. The use of many different techniques by the speech clinician will provide greater success. The application of one technique to all retarded children is not desirable.

9. Careful measures of language and speech abilities should be made at the beginning of therapy and at regular intervals throughout the therapy program.

10. The goals for the retarded child should be socially useful and appropriate communication skills commensurate with his mental age.

Such general principles can be applied to the various situations in which the speech clinician may be called upon to provide speech and language therapy. Also, they should be applied to the various levels of retarded individuals. As with any set of guidelines that might be stated, all of them will not fit every situation, but they should provide a basis for developing specific guides for specific programs.

Communication in the home

The puzzling question of when to begin speech and language therapy is a difficult one to answer in relation to the mentally retarded child. Generally, it has been found that direct therapy is not very effective with a child whose mental age has not reached 3 years. Considering some of the aspects of speech and language development discussed previously, this approach would seem to be logical and efficient. However, much valuable time is lost, particularly with the retarded child, if nothing is done prior to the initiation of direct therapy.

Most speech clinicians have come to believe that some responsibility for providing indirect speech and language therapy rests with the home before a child is ready for direct therapy. Ideally this kind of management should begin as soon as the diagnosis of mental retardation is completed. However, parents vary greatly in their ability to accept and adjust to the fact that their child is retarded. In some instances, the speech clinician would be wise to wait until the parents show acceptance of the more basic problem of retardation before confronting them with ways of stimulating speech and language development.

If a home program is to be effective, parents should be eager to participate and be able to recognize the child's present level of communication abilities. If they insist that a child is functioning at a higher level, or if they intend to make him function at his chronological age level, the job of the speech clinician is to help them understand the realities of the situation before involving them in a program to stimulate language. It appears clinically to be almost a universal tendency on the part of parents to attempt to push the retarded child beyond his capabilities. For this reason, the clinician must go to great lengths to explain to the parents the limits of the child's capabilities, especially in terms of mental age and other limiting factors, if they are present.

Early training of the parents in methods of motivation, stimulation, feedback, and insight concerning the development of communication cannot be overemphasized. Progress will be slow and probably will keep pace with the rate of mental development. If parents are to continue to stimulate a child at the proper level of development, much encouragement from the consulting speech clinician is likely to be needed. This is true because it takes so much longer for the mentally retarded child to move from one level of development to another. If parents have other older children, their pattern of stimulation may be based on a "normal" rate or if they have no other children, they may not understand the stages of language development very well.

Another factor that may result in parents' failing to provide the proper language stimulation is the unresponsiveness of the retarded child. As a general rule, the retarded child requires many more repetitions of an activity or many more stimulations before he responds as would the nonretarded child. Unless parents understand this, they frequently stop responding to the child because they are not getting adequate feedback to keep them interested in stimulating him. They may react by moving to a higher level of stimulation, which makes it impossible for the retarded child to respond. With proper counseling, they can drop back to an earlier level of language development and satisfy their need for responsiveness from the child, then continue to stimulate at the level the child should acquire next. Needless to say, this requires that the speech clinician be thoroughly familiar with the stages of language development and be quite skilled at evaluating the early stages.

The speech clinician who is not very familiar with early vocalizations of infants will find the work of Rheingold (75) quite helpful. She has shown that the human being provokes more social responses from infants than any other object and her descriptions of ways to increase these social responses and vocalizations will provide valuable information for use in counseling parents of retarded infants.

Before the child is ready for direct speech training, it is also necessary to give much attention to the requisites for developing speech and language. These aspects have been discussed in an earlier chapter, but their importance is great enough to be mentioned again here. Particularly in instances in which diagnosis of mental retardation can be made shortly after birth, as in mongolism, it is essential to work carefully with parents so that they keep pace with the developmental levels as a child progresses. It is not wise to describe specific things to tell parents or to suggest specific activities, because each set of parents and each child is so different. Rather, the speech clinician should spend enough time with each set of parents to answer their specific questions, to see ways of helping them manage their problems related to communication, and to help them develop ways of sustaining interaction between them and their mentally retarded child.

By 3 months of age, the normal infant has developed some rather specific patterns of responding to his environment and of seeking stimulation in his environment. This means that the retarded child is likely to develop some of these patterns during his first year, and a significant number of parents will need guidance in helping to develop these patterns of exploratory behavior and observing the responses. In some instances, parents and speech clinicians will need to recognize that children can become unresponsive if too much stimulation is constantly aimed at them. In other instances, it is important to remember that no amount of highly skilled stimulation and motivation will bring about development of communication skills ahead of the child's capacity for these skills. The most important thing for all concerned with guiding the development of early communication skills is that each child must progress at his own rate, and the best stimulation should be directed at his present level and the next successive level.

Communication in the school

There is considerable variation in school policies relative to providing speech therapy to children in special classes. The speech clinician must work within the limitations of these policies. Very frequently, other demands on the time of the speech clinician will encourage him to seek improvement in communication skills of the retarded child by working with the classroom teacher and the parents instead of with the child. With the trainable mentally retarded, in particular, progress may be so slow in proportion to the amount of time the speech clinician can give that he must rely primarily on the home, classroom, or whatever situation the child may be in. This has the advantage of providing the necessary communication experiences throughout the major portion of the day rather than during specific "speech-improvement" periods only.

Matthews (67) has suggested that perhaps use of procedures developed in speech-improvement programs in many schools will be more appropriate than individual speech therapy for the retarded child. When such programs have functioned adequately, the speech clinician has worked in close cooperation with the classroom teacher in developing general speech improvement activities that include all children in a classroom, but that can be geared to those specific individuals in need of more concentrated help.

The tendency of many clinicians to keep parents well in the background with respect to speech therapy, and to communicate somewhat sparingly with them concerning what is being done, needs to be completely eliminated in dealing with the mentally retarded. However, even when the clinician is inclined to involve the parents as much as possible, it becomes very difficult in many school situations. In some, he is not allowed to make home visits, he cannot schedule sufficient time for parent training, and it may be very difficult to get teachers and administrators to understand that a good portion of the time he spends with a child could be better spent with the parents.

For those clinicians working in school systems in which there are special classes for the retarded, parents need to be brought into the therapy program as much as possible —individually and in groups. If group parent training sessions can be organized, this is highly desirable. These should not be just parent discussion groups, but parent training sessions. In them, the clinician will give parents a good understanding of the normal development of language and speech, of methods of grossly assessing communication levels of their children, of the levels at which their children are functioning, and then specific techniques for stimulation and communication experience at these levels. Fortunately, there are good materials to assist the clinician and parents in this kind of training, such as that of Kirk, Karnes, and Kirk (51) and others listed in the source materials in the supplementary references.

Regardless of the specific school situation, a number of techniques and activities have been found to be very useful. Clinicians have used many of these methods in handling other kinds of speech problems. A very helpful guide has been provided by Freeman and Lukens (22). These authors have described a program for educable mentally retarded children that has proved to be highly successful in a public school system. The description of this program has several significant aspects as follow:

Speech and language must be taught as part of the regular classroom curriculum to meet the needs of those children whose retardation in these areas is one aspect of total developmental delay. . . . It is the responsibility of classroom teachers to cooperate in the formulation and execution of a curriculum for oral communication. This curriculum must: a) Provide opportunities to stimulate the entire class with appropriate language patterns; b) Meet the needs of children with delayed articulation development; c) Provide carry-over situations for children enrolled in speech correction classes.

It is obvious that such a basis for a communication program for the mentally retarded brings the speech clinician and the classroom teacher into a single program, and places the major activity designed to improve the communication skills of the children in the classroom where there is full daytime supervision of the child. As the article states: "The dynamic atmosphere of the classroom provides a continuous stream of opportunities that may be seized upon as vehicles for the situational-type therapy." Some of these opportunities are described as structuring the situation so that the class has particular responses to make during roll call, or when passing out papers, or when receiving materials, etc.

The program progresses systematically from highly structured initial verbal activities requiring the use of specific responses to more loosely structured situations that allow more opportunity for the child to initiate verbal responses as he improves, and, finally, to free role playing. It is stressed that initially the verbal situations need to be highly structured, even though they are real-life situations built around reception and expression of those verbal activities most encountered and most useful in the child's social relationships. Along with this, the authors state that there must be "extremely frequent repetition of meaningful communication experiences." This program seems to have been able to avoid routine drill, yet provide a great deal of necessary repetition by the use of well-motivated useful social situations.

The activities centering around real and synthetic life situations recommended by Freeman and Lukens (22) and many others always must be designed to accomplish certain specific purposes. These are summarized by Harrison (32) as: "1) Listening; 2) Following directions; 3) Making wants known; 4) Recognizing symbols; 5) Oral communication." The alert clinician will find many activities that can be adapted to accomplish these specific goals. Listening skills, for example, can be developed through story-telling, simple dialogue, games designed to bring responses based on accurate listening, and radio and TV programs if they are carefully selected.

For the development of oral expression, choral reading has been recommended widely as it gives the child an opportunity to be somewhat "lost" in the group while making verbal responses.

Schlanger (79) gives an example of activities that appear to be very useful. For the development of sensory perception he suggests the use of rhythm band instruments, sounds made by self, and sounds made by external sources such as cars, bells, birds, and animals. The child may move in time to music, march, clap, circle, and imitate instruments, or he may listen to story-telling, nursery rhymes, songs, point to pictures, and turn pages. For the development of expressive behavior Schlanger suggests stimulating conversation by permitting the child to act out feelings using rubber dolls representing family figures, farm animals, clay, coloring crayons and finger paints, doll house and furniture, naming things such as parts of the body, clothing, book and magazine pictures, memory games using objects, and the use of creative drama built around nursery rhymes or parties, as well as social situations using stereotyped phrases. He suggests the use of records accompanied by actions named by the clinician, and the use of card games adapted to speech and sentence development, such as the Bryngelson-Glaspey picture cards, Old Maid, Simon Says, etc., and the use of a number of sound-discrimination games.

Irwin (41) has described a number of specific techniques and materials helpful to parents in articulation training. The clinician also may find some use for this material, although generally he will have available articulation training material that he has used previously with other children having articulation problems, and which will be suitable for the mentally retarded.

A great deal of stress has been placed on the value of group and other social situations in communication therapy with the mentally retarded. It must be realized, however, that there are a number of exceptions to this kind of procedure. One of these factors concerns the child whose language progresses to a reasonably adequate stage, but who continues to make isolated articulation errors or to exhibit voice or other problems that might yield to correction. If the child has reached such a communication level, and if there are no contraindications from the standpoint of organic involvement of the speech organs, the speech probably also can be improved considerably. In such a case, individual articulation therapy might be the best procedure—and certainly a time-saver.

Another exception to the group situation may be the retarded "brain-damaged" individual whose stimulation threshold is so low that he is unable to function adequately in a group or in highly stimulating social situations. For this child a highly structured, protected individual situation may be the best choice. Likewise, the child with a major crippling condition, such as cerebral palsy, may find it extremely difficult to fit into almost any kind of social group, although such a situation might well be best for him. In such cases, if it is not possible to integrate him into a group, individual therapy might produce desirable results.

Finally, as with all group therapy, most individuals involved in the therapeutic situation need periods of individual attention from the teacher or clinician. Opportunity should be provided for this individual attention to each child on different occasions, if it is at all possible. This session may be no more than a brief get-acquainted period, a time for conversation, a time for very intensive practice of a particularly needed exercise, or an extended period of counseling.

What we are suggesting is a principle that holds true in any kind of therapy, which is: While one particular approach generally might appear to be most suitable for the retarded, the clinician always must reserve the right to alter this approach, to disagree with it if he finds other approaches better, and to substitute his own procedures when he feels the need. Such procedures, however, should be based on the individual differences and needs of the child rather than on clinical biases or an unwillingness to develop new patterns of therapy procedure.

Communication in a mental institution

As we stated in earlier chapters, the majority of the retardates in institutions are in the custodial or trainable groups. In the custodial group, almost all will have inadequate communication skills and many will be almost entirely nonverbal. Although most institutionalized retardates will have limited verbal skills even under ideal stimulation and circumstances, they also need to be helped to reach their potential in communication, self-care, and productivity. The speech clinician working with such individuals will need to give careful consideration to the establishment of realistic goals and will need to take advantage of all situations in which communication with the retardate would be appropriate. The Parsons Project (78) pointed out that the caretakers and aides working with such retardates often perform their duties without any verbal communication taking place. This kind of situation must be changed if all avenues of help available are to be utilized.

One of the responsibilities of the speech clinician working in an institutional setting, then, might be to find ways of encouraging the staff to talk to the retardates at a level that can be understood. Here, as in other instances, the evaluation of communication skills and the establishment of levels of these skills will help the speech clinician to develop with the staff the kind of communication that will be meaningful to the retardate. As most individuals would see little value in talking to a 22-year-old retardate as if he were 2 years old (which may be his language level), the staff working in this situation will require some instruction, some reinforcement from the speech clinician, and some evaluation of the effects of such efforts. Specific techniques for accomplishing these objectives are not well known, but it seems reasonable that starting to communicate at the level the retardate can understand is the first step. The difficulty is in making the experience meaningful to the staff person so he will continue to communicate with the retardate who naturally will not share ideas or be able to respond in a way that will be challenging to the individual staff member.

The problem of justification of therapy for the institutionalized retardate is a marked one. Usually there is such a wide range of capabilities in an institutional population that it will be worthwhile to do a great deal of screening and to establish speech and language levels and a prognosis for improvement before starting a therapy program. Even with the use of other staff members, there will not be enough help to go around; thus selections must be made from those retardates whose condition holds promise of some justifiable results.

Most good mental institutions today have a variety of programs and provide many different opportunities for their inmates. One of the best is an educational program or a "school" within the institution. In the better institutions, these schools are well-staffed, and many kinds of training at the individual's capacity level are offered. The speech clinician will find his most profitable expenditure of time among the children in the school setting of the institution, as they will be the most capable and the teaching staff of the school will be the most amenable to accepting help from the clinician by way of providing a rich speech and language stimulation situation.

The good institutions also provide different living arrangements. One of the most promising is the cottage style, in which groups of children are somewhat homogeneously selected to live in smaller groups in individual cottages under fairly close adult supervision. The cottage life itself provides opportunities for motivating and encouraging communication, and a group situation in which many techniques for speech and language stimulation may be developed.

Other institutions provide a nonresident situation in which patients are at the institution only during the daytime and at home (in the community) in the evenings. In these situations it is possible to utilize the family and the community in many of the ways suggested above to improve communication skills. While it is likely that children in this situation may have a little better communication skill than the institution's residential population, there will be many communication problems—but such children will also present a better prognosis for improvement.

Another situation that is found in some good institutions is that of team diagnosis and treatment. In this situation the speech clinician has the opportunity to assist and be assisted by specialists in medicine, dentistry, psychology, social work, occupational and physical therapy, nursing, and teaching in planning and carrying out speech and language therapy, both on an individual and a group basis. When this situation is present, the clinician should make every effort to help develop and use it to its fullest extent.

Finally, it must be pointed out that, although many mental institutions are now adding speech and hearing specialists to their staffs, the working situation still is far from ideal—and in many instances is very discouraging. A sympathetic understanding of the institution's procedures and problems is highly important. The opportunities offered in such a situation are numerous and exciting if an individual has the imagination and creativity to take advantage of them. Approached in a positive, objective manner, this situation could be one that would provide great satisfaction to the communication specialist and, at the same time, result in considerable assistance to children who are much in need of such assistance.

Communication in the clinic

Clinically, it has been noted that if a child is not talking well by 3 years of age, parents seek evaluation and help. They may start with their physician or they may go directly to a community or college speech and hearing clinic. After thorough evaluation and diagnosis, the speech clinician working in such a setting must decide whether speech therapy is indicated. Rather than assuming that a specific chronological or mental age indicates the time for beginning direct therapy, a communication level should be established. When this level approaches that of a normal 3-year-old child, specific therapy approaches may be made, especially with respect to developing language structure and concepts. From there on, the therapy can be expanded and increased according to the individual child's development and along the lines to be suggested in this chapter.

Articulation therapy certainly would not be instituted

at this point, and perhaps for a number of years thereafter. If the retarded child is not likely to develop connected speech until 2 or 4 years after it normally should occur, and perhaps some sort of usable sentence structure from 2 to 4 or 5 years after that time, attempts at refinement of the sounds and words he uses so imperfectly at earlier ages would be pointless. Articulation therapy, then, should be based upon the language development level. The optimum mental or chronological age will vary with each child, but will be late for all.

With the nonretarded child, the speech clinician is not likely to do much to improve the articulation directly or to encourage the parents to interfere with the articulation before the time when the child is using fairly complete 3- and 4-word sentences with a vocabulary of several hundred words. It would be even more confusing to begin the refinement of articulation ability earlier than at this stage with the retarded child. If it is evident that the child has sufficient language to understand concrete ideas of others and to attempt to express his own concrete ideas, some help in making these expressions more intelligible is indicated regardless of the age at which this level of communication skill is reached.

Almost all clinicians and experimenters who have dealt extensively with communication problems of the mentally retarded agree with the principle already mentioned that language therapy must precede articulation therapy. One of the best ways to achieve improvement in communication skills of the retarded is through group social experience aimed at developing the need for verbal communication as a means of relating to and expressing this experience. This procedure has been described in various ways. Perhaps one of the most extensive research projects bearing on this general principle was that of Lassers and Low (53), which concluded, in part:

1) The speech of mentally retarded children can be improved through speech training.

2) Speech proficiency of mentally retarded children can be more effectively improved with an approach based on duplication of real-life experiences ("communication-centered speech therapy") than with a drill-type ("conventional speech therapy") approach to speech training.

3) The degree of speech improvement of the educable mentally retarded is greater than that of severely mentally retarded as a result of the two major types of speech training used in the investigation.

Lassers and Low based these conclusions on a 4-month period of intensive therapy, in which they used the two types of approaches mentioned above. They found that in a 4-month period of therapy the communication-centered speech therapy improved articulation more effectively than the conventional approach, but that both types of therapy improved oral grammatical complexity of the mentally retarded in comparison with the control group that had no therapy. They suggest that the results of their study give strong support to the integration of training in communication skills with daily life activities in the home, classroom, and elsewhere.

One might object to the assumption on the part of Lassers and Low that what they call "conventional speech therapy" consists primarily of "drill." It is doubtful that the competent speech clinician today relies to any great extent on drill for the improvement of speech and language. Rather, he is more likely to be found using a wide variety of motivational processes based on the child's social life and the immediate environmental situations. Even the direct clinically contrived motivational materials at the clinician's command are likely not to be of the drill type, but will be highly varied and stimulating.

For these reasons, it is believed that most speech clinicians will be well-qualified to use communication-centered therapy with the mentally retarded as they do with many other kinds of problems. What the speech clinician must do with the retarded is to integrate the home, school, and community experiences with clinical activity. There is a tendency in speech and language therapy for the clinician to work in relative isolation from the child's total environment. This is especially true in many clinical programs because of limitations of schedules, case load, space, time, and other factors. However, it is seldom that the speech clinician can give enough time to complete the task of developing communication skills of retarded individuals. Without the help of all who associate with the retardate, the enormous task of developing speech and language moves at a discouragingly slow rate.

One possible reason for the poor results reported regarding speech therapy with retarded individuals has been pointed out by Matthews (67). He said:

An examination of the various suggestions for speech therapy for the mentally retarded indicates that many of the recommended procedures might be difficult to carry out in the traditional one-or-two-sessions-per-week kind of individual speech therapy offered in many clinics. Much of the suggested speech correction program may not be carried out by the speech therapist but by parents, teachers, and others who spend considerable time with the retarded child. Perhaps the pessimism about the success of speech therapy with the mentally retarded is based to a large extent on the failure to apply to the retarded therapy procedures suited to their needs and capacities.

Another approach to the development of speech and language in retarded individuals that has met with considerable success is operant conditioning. Many approaches to the application of operant conditioning principles are possible. One of the most useful is that in which Lovaas *et al.* (61) demonstrated the acquisition of imitative speech in 2 mute schizophrenic children with the use of operant conditioning principles. This approach would be equally valuable with mentally retarded children. The training procedure they employed consisted of four distinct steps that should be clinically useful in planning speech or language therapy for retarded children utilizing operant principles. The four steps described by Lovaas *et al.* (61) are:

1. Increase the free operant rate of vocalization; the child was reinforced for all vocalization.

2. Temporal discrimination; the child was reinforced only if he vocalized within 6 seconds after an adult's vocalization.

3. Matching; in this step the child was required to match the adult's vocalization by successive approximation.

4. Discrimination; the child was required to discriminate between the sounds.

As retarded children frequently fail to engage in imitative behavior spontaneously, time spent establishing imitative vocalizations might prove very profitable in developing language and speech skills. The program of specific reinforcement must be continued until the speech and language behavior can be sustained through the usual patterns of social reinforcement. Otherwise, the retarded child feels that primary reinforcers (usually food) should be forthcoming each time he communicates appropriately. This is a clinical approach or technique that requires close cooperation of the parents and others in the child's environment. It is more effective if all individuals associated with the child understand the goals and the step of the program being used at a particular time.

Whenever the speech clinician finds the opportunity and thinks it appropriate to work directly with the communication of the retarded child, he should make every effort to arrange therapy sessions so that they are frequent, are built primarily around group experiences, and allow for a great deal of variety in activities. This variety should include a wide range of social experiences that allow for such things as trips to the store and walks around the block or into the park. Also, it is wise to utilize a great deal of motivational material both audio and visual— that is, tape recorders, film strips, moving pictures, and a large variety of toys and simple work tools.

The usual twice-a-week, 15-minute or ½-hr. therapy period, individually or in small groups, is least desirable —although it may be the best that the clinician can do because of limitations of his situation. Certainly, a wise selection of patients may offer opportunity for even this kind of a limited program to meet with some success. Many situations also will not allow for the flexibility in facilities and materials mentioned above, so that the clinician will need to use a great deal of creative imagination both with respect to collecting materials and developing appropriate activities.

Related communication problems

In addition to the communication problems related most directly to the mental retardation is the fact that the retarded child will be subject to any of the communication disorders that may be found in any other child. In some cases the retardate is more prone to these problems simply because of the totality of his retardation. The speech and hearing specialist dealing with the retarded in whatever setting may expect to find retarded children who stutter, who have cleft lip and palate, who have cerebral palsy, who have dysphasia, who show articulatory errors not related to the retardation, and whose speech and language have been delayed or made deviant because of hearing loss or deafness. These problems must be diagnosed and treated in the retarded as they would in the nonretarded.

The factor of retardation, however, adds a serious dimension to communication problems. For example, the child with cerebral palsy who also is severely retarded may present a much poorer prognosis than if the same child had normal intelligence. The neuromuscular and sometimes symbolic problems of the cerebral palsied are difficult, at best, but with a child who is lacking in intelligence and motivation for improvement, the task of assisting him may be near hopeless.

The child with a cleft palate may profit a great deal from extended procedures beyond the basic repair if he possesses all of the other necessary attributes. If his speech and language are severely delayed because of retardation, or if there is a neuromuscular retardation or deficiency or any of the other problems known to accompany retardation, it may be that the extended procedures are not indicated. Careful consideration would be required regarding fitting a prosthetic speech appliance for a retarded child with hypernasal voice quality. In such an instance, one would have to evaluate the child's capability of understanding the usefulness of the appliance and his ability to care for it. The same may be said of the retarded child who needs a hearing aid.

The dysphasic retarded child presents an additional problem. As his basic problem is one of failure to master adequate use of the symbols of language, he presents initially an almost impossible problem when the dysphasic element of symbolic disorganization is superimposed. The retarded child who stutters likewise presents a difficult problem because the treatment of stuttering depends a great deal on the individual's ability to comprehend, at a fairly abstract level, the psychological principles of self-management in relation to the stuttering problem. The nonretarded child usually can begin to develop a fairly accurate self-concept necessary for successful treatment of stuttering in his early teens. The retardate may be much later in developing this capacity, or he may not develop it at all. This means that procedures for treating the stuttering problem may need to be at a much more concrete mechanical level than is necessary for the nonretarded secondary stutterer.

On the other hand, the retarded child has so much against him that if there is a chance of improving his communication such therapy should not be neglected. When, after careful evaluation of the total situation, it is determined that there is some reasonable hope for progress, the retarded child with cerebral palsy, cleft palate, stuttering, etc., should be given every chance to succeed—and whatever procedures are necessary in the management of the problem should be taken.

Management of these other conditions that result in communication problems should proceed along the same lines with the retarded as with the nonretarded, with adjustments being made as necessary to accommodate for the many other problems related to the retardation. Therapy goals in such cases may need to be much less ambitious than they would for the nonretarded, and the possibility of considerable discouragement and frustration should be considered. At the same time, if the goals are realistic and the management is the best that can be obtained, progress may be quite rewarding.

As has been pointed out earlier, hearing problems are from three to four times more prevalent among the retarded than the nonretarded. The effect of loss of hearing on the development of speech and language in any child is well known; the effect on the retarded child is greatly amplified because of his limited capacity to compensate for the lack of hearing acuity. For example, the intelligent child with a hearing loss begins very early to search faces and other aspects of his environment for clues as to the meaning of sounds around him, including speech. The process of searching for and learning to use these clues is a complicated one, and demands a fairly high level of intelligence and capacity for abstraction. The retarded child is deficient in both these areas. He usually will be much more likely to put forth less effort to understand what he is hearing, and may not try so hard to reproduce it. It is a common experience in any educational situation for the deaf that the retarded child is extremely limited in his capacity to learn to read lips, or even to learn sign language. In many cases, the abstractness of a symbol system is entirely beyond the capacity of the retarded child. The degree of deficiency will depend largely on the degree of retardation and accompanying environmental conditions.

In spite of these severe limitations, the hard-of-hearing or the deaf retarded child should have every opportunity available if there is any hope of helping him to communicate better. Certainly the educable retarded, especially in the upper ranges, can profit from the same therapy procedures as used for the nonretarded hard-of-hearing child. This is true also of the retarded deaf. In this same group also there will be considerable success from providing an adequate hearing aid when it is indicated and when adequate training in the use of the aid and in auditory stimulation and speech therapy are available.

The same management procedures, then, for the hard-of-hearing retarded child should be used as for the nonretarded, with the added precaution that provision be made for the likely intensification of the difficulty in the retarded, and the necessity for simplified, concrete, and repeated therapy procedures.

Summary

From the above discussion it may be seen that the management of communication problems in the retarded child is an extremely complicated task that requires a high degree of initiative and creativity as well as endless patience on the part of the speech and hearing specialist. Basic to any success in management of these problems is a high degree of competence, beginning first with a thorough knowledge of the normal processes of speech and language development, the factors that disrupt this development, the disorders that result, and the effects of these disorders—not only on a normal child but on the retarded as well. The latter aspect demands a great deal of understanding of the nature of retardation and the sources from which one may draw support and assistance in therapy for the communication disorders.

It requires a high degree of versatility and skill in human relations as well as skill as a professional speech pathologist or audiologist to make maximum use of the home environment, the community, the school, the various facets of the institution, and all of the resources of the clinic in the successful management of the speech and language development and therapy for the retarded child. No other therapeutic process carries a greater challenge to the speech pathologist and audiologist than this area. The need is great, and the contribution can be significant if the challenge is successfully met.

Supplemental references

Brindle, F. "The Teaching of Language to the Educationally Subnormal." *Slow-Learning Child,* Vol. 10, 1963. Pp. 47–52.

Dowd, Ann Helen. "The Role of Speech Therapy in the Personality Development of the Mentally Retarded Child." *The Bulletin,* Georgetown University Medical Center, Vol. 11, No. 5, 1958.

Hahn, E. "Communication in the Therapy Session: A Point of View." *Journal of Speech and Hearing Disorders,* Vol. 25, 1960. Pp. 18–23.

Irwin, Ruth Becky. "Oral Language for Slow-Learning Children." *American Journal of Mental Deficiency,* Vol. 64, No. 1, 1959. Pp. 32–40.

Kastein, S. "The Responsibility of the Speech Pathologist to the Retarded Child." *American Journal of Mental Deficiency,* Vol. 60, No. 4, 1956. Pp. 750–754.

McCarthy, J. J. "Linguistic Problems of the Retarded." *Mental Retardation Abstracts,* Vol. 1, 1964. Pp. 3–27.

McCarthy, J. J. "The Importance of Linguistic Ability in the Mentally Retarded." *Mental Retardation,* Vol. 2, 1964. Pp. 90–96.

Mecham, M. J., and L. J. Jex. "Training Mentally Retarded Children in Oral Communication." *ASHA,* Vol. 4, No. 12, 1962. Pp. 441–443.

Smith, J. O. "Group Language Development for Educable Mental Retardates." *Exceptional Children,* Vol. 29, No. 2, 1962. Pp. 95–101.

Wood, Nancy E. *Language Disorders in Children.* Chicago, National Society for Crippled Children and Adults, 1959. Pp. 21–31.

CHAPTER 8

Therapy procedures for communication disorders

In an earlier chapter, discussion centered around the need for careful evaluation of the basic processes involved in speech, language, and hearing. Information gained from those assessments, viewed in relation to background, educational history, psychological factors, and the behavioral status of the individual serves as the basis for planning specific therapeutic procedures. So many precise facts are needed in relation to a specific individual that it is extremely difficult to describe in a meaningful way techniques and procedures that are universally effective for modifying speech and language behavior.

Most clinicians working with retarded children have

an ability to simplify instructions and to converse with the retarded individual at the patient's current level of language function. However, sometimes attempts to modify linguistic behavior fail because instructions are too complicated—not because the procedures are faulty. A reasonable rule to follow is that specific instructions for a retarded child should be stated in language that is at or near the same level of complexity that the retardate previously has demonstrated ability to understand. Often the retarded individual is confused by too much verbal instruction and too little opportunity to practice skills himself. The statement that "nothing succeeds like success" has much meaning in working with the retarded individual. Expectations that are within the capability of the individual, and reward for achieving the expected goal or a close approximation of it will do a great deal to develop willingness to try new tasks and to persist until a task is accomplished.

Respiration

Modification of respiratory function, which is so basic to control of the other processes related to expressive speech, has received too little attention from speech pathologists. Control of the exhalation phase obviously has considerable significance in speaking. Westlake (91) has discussed the need to phonate a vowel such as "ah" for 10 seconds as a minimum of expiratory control for connected speech. His work was with children who have cerebral palsy, but the findings would be just as appropriate for the retarded child. Some retarded individuals who use only the first syllable of words are unable to sustain phonation for more than 3 or 4 seconds. Most individuals can increase the time of sustained phonation by 1 or 2 seconds in a given session when they are given encouragement and some visible recognition of their efforts.

The importance of breathing through the nose rather than the mouth is based on the physiological purpose of the nose—its function is to warm and filter the air before it hits the posterior wall of the pharynx. If this action does not occur, the mucosal tissues of the tongue, oral cavity, and pharynx become dry and sometimes irritated. In addition to effecting better physiological functioning, the appearance of the retarded individual is improved considerably by having the lips closed in the usual manner. When nonretarded individuals imitate the retarded, the first action may be to open the mouth and push the tongue forward. Forward carriage of the tongue by individuals who are mouth breathers probably occurs because of an attempt to warm and moisten the air with the tongue. The benefits of establishing nasal breathing patterns are numerous for the retarded child.

Before any attempts to teach nasal breathing are made, the speech clinician should have assurance from a physician that there is no nasal obstruction that would interfere with nasal breathing. There are many ways of encouraging this activity. Some children respond to praise for keeping lips together for a few seconds at a time and are able gradually to increase the time. Others will keep lips together for 5 minutes in order to obtain a penny, a piece of candy, or some other item of their choice. Parents may be capable of and interested in assisting, and may accomplish most of the job at home. Episodes of upper-respiratory infection frequently will re-establish mouth breathing after an individual has fairly adequate patterns of respiration. It is important to regain the nasal breathing as soon after nasal congestion is cleared as is possible.

Modification of poor posture associated with poor patterns of respiration comes through direct instruction and reward for responses. It can be started with quite young children by encouraging their imitation of adults or older brothers or sisters. Games can be used with adequate performance being praised and rewarded. "Head erect" and "shoulders square" are the goals. Achievement of better posture results in more adequate inhalation and exhalation.

The problem of speaking on inhalation sometimes will be found among the retarded. Very few speakers phonate on inhalation consistently, but occasionally a child will produce one or two sounds during inhalation. Most of the time it is necessary to establish ability to produce the affected sound in isolation on exhaled air before attempting to modify its use in words or sentences. Holding a paper in front of the speaker's lips and getting him to imitate the examiner's production of the sound that makes the paper move may help develop a feeling for sound production on exhalation. Other children respond more to the feel of air on their own hand (instead of the movement of the paper). Once the problem sounds are learned, their use in words can be established by practice and recognition of the correct usage. Adequate control of exhalation also helps alleviate the problem of speaking on inhalation.

Situations in which most of the breath supply is lost before phonation occurs sometimes is noticed among the retarded. There seems to be a lack of coordination between the respiratory process and the phonatory process. This is a difficult problem to modify because explanations of it are not understood easily by the retarded individual. The more effective procedures have been directed at signaling the child to phonate just before inhalation is complete. Careful observation by the speech pathologist can determine when the phonation is occurring with better breath supply. When phonation is more adequate, this improvement should be treated as success, and practice can be continued until the individual can phonate consistently without losing too much air.

The oral manometer has been quite useful in enabling retarded children to develop more adequate oral breath pressure. Most of them can get the idea that the needle on the dials is supposed to go farther for a better score. They will work at taking a deep breath in order to blow into the manometer and see the dial move. Various toys that are dependent on blowing for their function sometimes are useful in controlling exhalation.

Many retarded children function adequately with regard to respiratory function as it relates to speaking. Some of them demonstrate the problems described in this section and others that are not described. Whatever the problem, it should be dealt with directly—with little intellectualizing about it when working with the retarded individual.

Phonation

Phonatory problems are those associated with laryngeal dysfunction. One of the most frequent problems is that of a harsh voice associated with too much tension of the vocal folds. Any method of reducing tension appropriate to the mental age level of the individual is effective in improving voice quality that is poor because of tension. Head rolling, chewing, or jaw shaking all have been used successfully. The major difference in using these methods with the retarded individual is that the speech pathologist depends more on imitation than explanation of the purpose of the exercise. Many retarded children will be able to reduce the tenseness without understanding exactly what they are doing.

Breathiness, which results from improper movement of the vocal folds, often is best modified through altering loudness of the voice. The extra effort to use more volume results in quicker and more adequate movements of the vocal folds, thus eliminating the breathy component. This may be accomplished by various methods, but imitation of the loudness level desired again seems to be the most reliable procedure.

Hoarseness is a frequent problem among retarded individuals. It may be associated with several laryngeal problems described in the chapter on diagnosis of communication problems. The only cause of hoarseness that the speech pathologist may be able to modify is vocal abuse, which may result from yelling, improper pattern of phonation, or from speaking with too much tension of the vocal folds. Wilson (92) has described several techniques that are appropriate for treating hoarseness in retarded individuals. Again, it is important to demonstrate what the individual must accomplish and not provide too much verbal explanation. Modification of any activity that results in abuse of the vocal folds is very important and can be accomplished only through taking a careful history of vocal activity and having the cooperation of the parents in changing activities thought to be associated with hoarseness.

Abnormal pitch of the voice (i.e., too low or too high) is not a frequent problem with retarded individuals. When it does occur, it may be related to physical dimensions of the vocal folds and therefore may not be changed through training. Attempts to change the habitual pitch of the voice should be carried out only if the speech pathologist has assurance that the individual can modify habitual pitch without causing other phonatory problems such as hoarseness. As modification of pitch requires considerable self-direction, many retarded individuals are unable to accomplish it before young adulthood.

Most pitch problems become more noticeable after the usual voice change at puberty. For this reason, immediately after puberty the child has reached a good age level to attempt to develop appropriate pitch. Determination of optimum pitch is the first step, and encouragement to use that pitch follows. The speech clinician usually finds it necessary to help monitor the pitch until the individual becomes thoroughly familiar with the new pitch. If the new pitch is to be used effectively, the retarded individual must learn to recognize it himself and to know when he is using it. This is accomplished through imitation and practice.

Examples of phonatory problems and ways in which they have been modified would serve little purpose in this discussion. Each one is different and each must be studied in relation to the individual who has the problem. If such problems are approached in this manner, the speech pathologist is free to try any technique that fits the given situation. Careful observation of the results will determine if the effort should be continued or if another method should be used.

Resonation

The resonance of any individual's voice is determined predominantly by the size and shape of the resonating cavities; therefore, there is little that the speech pathologist can alter. However, there are a number of factors associated with articulation that have some influence; one of them is the degree of movement of the mandible. If an individual talks without moving his mandible, less area of the oral cavity can serve as resonating space. This may result in a muffling that does not allow clear sounds and may reduce intelligibility of the person's speech. It is relatively easy to modify this problem by instructing the individual to open his mouth more while speaking, and reinforcing him for doing this.

The second major problem of resonance involves the nasal cavity, the nasopharynx, and the soft palate. As discussed in other chapters, if the soft palate does not contact the posterior wall of the pharynx, too much sound enters the nasal cavity and hypernasality results. This situation influences not only resonance but articulation as well. Hypernasality and the weak consonant articulation associated with it has been reported in 21 percent of the children seen in the multidiscipline mental retardation program at the University of Oregon Medical School (65). The problem occurs frequently enough that speech pathologists should be aware of ways to deal with it.

The primary responsibility of the speech pathologist is to identify the problem and then recommend evaluations and procedures that will modify structures so that adequate palatopharyngeal closure is provided. Basically, three methods—exercise, surgical procedures, prosthetic devices—have been used to achieve adequate palatopharyngeal closure. All of these methods have been successful in specific individuals, yet the guidelines for choosing the most effective one for any individual are still unclear. Naturally, some of the decision depends upon the specialists available for consultation and upon cooperative work with the speech pathologist.

Numerous exercises for strengthening the soft palate have been described in the literature. However, the effectiveness of such exercises is highly questionable. If the problem actually is caused by habitually poor movement of the soft palate, exercises might result in some improvement. More often, poor palate movement is associated with a capacious pharynx, a submucous cleft of the soft or hard palate, a short soft palate, or isolated paralysis of the soft palate. In such instances, exercises seldom are effective in improving voice quality. Even when good voice quality is achieved, it requires so much effort from the individual that it may not last very long.

Results from the various surgical procedures available to produce more adequate palatopharyngeal closure have been poorer with retarded individuals than with those of normal intelligence. In fact, low intelligence has been stated as the cause for poor results from surgical procedures such as pharyngeal flap. The reasons for this are not clear, and research to determine the extent of improvement, or lack of it, following surgical intervention is not available at this time. Probably these surgical procedures should be used for individuals in the mildly retarded range until more is known about their effectiveness with moderately retarded individuals.

Speech appliances have been used quite successfully with nonretarded children as young as 3 years, and they can be made for retarded children who have achieved a mental age of approximately 3 years. Because younger children appear to achieve more gains with speech appliances than older ones, it is desirable to use the speech appliance as soon as it is evident that one is needed.

The speech pathologist and the parents should know how to remove and insert the speech appliance. Many retarded children learn to manage these devices quickly and efficiently, but initially adults need to assume the responsibility of placing and removing the speech appliance. Sometimes it is better for the child not to know how to remove it until he is accustomed to wearing it and has accepted its use. Some children fail to wear their speech appliance because mother or speech pathologist frown or grimace while inserting it, thus setting a negative attitude for the child. Most children accept a speech appliance without resistance if the adults involved accept it in the same manner.

Some programs involving speech appliances fail because the speech pathologist and the dental specialist involved neglect the very necessary follow-up required for all patients. As long as an individual is wearing a speech appliance, the device should be routinely checked every 3 months—and more often if problems develop. The size and shape of the pharyngeal portion of the bulb may have to be modified to maintain the best resonance, and the wires adjusted to maintain the best retention. Time spent obtaining adequate fit and acceptance of a speech appliance is far more effective in obtaining adequate resonance than time spent with palate exercises.

The other problem of resonance involves hyponasality. This occurs when the sounds *m, n, ŋ,* normally resonated in the nasal cavity, are not resonated there. The usual causes are colds, allergies, or nasal obstructions. There is little the speech pathologist can do to modify these defects except to see that the retarded individual is helped to learn nasal cleanliness and receives adequate medical attention if it is needed.

Articulation

Articulation problems among the retarded are more numerous than in the general population. The errors are of the same nature and require the same careful analysis as in the general population. It is likely that the most serious error speech pathologists make in articulation therapy with retarded individuals is that of beginning too soon. Often it is more appropriate to provide language development instruction than to attempt to provide articulation therapy. It would not be expected that an average 3-year-old would have accurate articulation of all sounds. Therefore, it should not be expected that the retarded child with a mental age of 3 years would have correct articulation of all English sounds. In fact, the articulation level often lags behind the mental age. The most important principle of articulation therapy is that of setting realistic goals consistent with the level of language development demonstrated by the retarded individual.

Methods of articulation therapy are numerous and each will be effective with some retarded individuals. Selection of the methods appropriate to the individual is important and can be done only in relation to the observed errors, the nature of these errors, and the response of the individual to attempts to modify them. A good clinician will have little trouble finding an effective therapy approach if he takes time to know the exact nature of the errors. A number of procedures that have been effective with nonretarded individuals, however, may not be adequate for use with the retarded.

Generally, with the retarded child, it is poor economy of time to attempt to develop sound discrimination for consonants in isolation. This activity appears to be so abstract that carry-over into better speech rarely occurs. Likewise, production of consonants in nonsense syllables or nonsense words usually is not effective therapy. Various approaches involving games with rules, scores, and motor activity are less effective with the retarded. It seems that these games become so involved that the retarded child is unable to remember the speech goals associated with them. Any technique that depends on the child's understanding an abstract, conceptual description of the activity will be difficult to use effectively. Things that appeal to the speech pathologist as "fun to do" often are too complicated for the retarded child. Any plan of therapy that moves in large steps usually confuses the retarded child. Many more smaller steps are usually necessary.

In the section on diagnosis, we mentioned the difficulty in the production of tongue-tip sounds such as *t* and *d*. Developing these sounds with nonretarded children often has been accomplished by showing the individual where the tongue should be placed and providing strong auditory stimulation or a strong auditory pattern for him to imitate. In the case of the retarded child, considerable time may be needed to teach him how to get his tongue to the proper place for production of these sounds. Tongue-tip elevation can sometimes be achieved by having the retarded child put his tongue just behind his upper front teeth, keeping it there, and lowering his jaw. This procedure may have to be repeated many times before it comes under voluntary control. Then the child may be able to place his tongue correctly, impound oral breath pressure, and release it for an adequate production of *t* and *d* sounds.

Among retarded children, it is not unusual to find poor control of tongue function that relates to articulation problems. Sometimes this difficulty is associated with poor patterns of chewing. In such instances it is necessary to attempt to modify chewing before attempting to establish tongue movements involved in sound production. Chewing a large bolus—such as two sticks of *sugarless* bubble gum, with lips closed—provides a great deal of tongue movement and muscle strengthening that may be beneficial in developing articulatory movements. Practice time for such activity should be increased from 1 to 5 minutes per day over a period of 4 or 5 weeks. It should be maintained for 2 or 3 months in order to permit development of adequate tongue movements.

Many retarded children use only the first syllable of multisyllable words; the reason for this is unclear and methods of modifying it are not specific and proved. It sometimes has been helpful to practice repetition of words such as "mama," "daddy," "baby," "no, no." This will help to establish ability to make repetitive sounds. Any word that the child says clearly can be used for such activity. Generalization of this ability to longer multisyllable words may not occur, but the practice may help to develop control of exhalation and to increase the ability to remember two or more syllables.

More and more speech pathologists are finding systematic planning and application of reinforcement principles from behavior modification to be effective in articulation therapy. Essentially this involves giving a reward of a tangible nature when the individual produces the sound correctly. (There is additional discussion of this principle at the end of this chapter.)

Symbolization

Efforts to deal with the linguistic symbolic aspects of language development in a therapeutic way are relatively recent. There is much that is not known about the ways in which language is acquired or learned. The retarded child who learns and repeats long commercials from TV programs, yet remains unable to use simple language effectively for communicating with others, baffles speech pathologists. The elements involved in understanding prepositions and personal pronouns are not clearly known. This makes language therapy difficult to plan and difficult to evaluate. Suggestions offered in this area can be only speculative at best. The guidelines are only tentative and subject to change as knowledge of the language learning process increases. The preceding chapter actually deals primarily with principles and procedures for language improvement. A few more specific suggestions may be useful here.

Imitation appears to play a major role in the development of language, both in expression and in comprehension. One of the problems in language therapy with retarded children has been that such children sometimes do not participate in imitative behavior. Studies by Baer, Peterson and Sherman (6) and by Lovaas (61) have demonstrated that imitation of nonverbal behavior can be established through reinforcement principles. These principles are not new to the speech pathologist, but their application on a carefully planned and tabulated basis is new to many. Extension of the imitative behavior—so that it comes under the control of stimuli similar to that met in real-life communication situations—still is under study, but progress is being made. Therapy of this nature appears to hold promise of being effective in developing communication skills. However, its ultimate success is dependent upon the individual's ability to generalize the skill acquired through imitation to new and different situations.

Little attention has been given to vicarious learning as a process that might facilitate the retarded child's ability to understand language and to use it effectively. As retarded children generally do learn television commercials, it seems worthwhile to explore the use of video tape as a teaching technique for developing useful language. Perhaps the repeated viewing of short segments of linguistic interchange of a meaningful nature, followed by opportunities to use such language appropriately, would be an efficient means of developing language concepts.

In establishing imitative behavior, Baer, Peterson, and Sherman (6) actually put the child through the desired action, provided immediate reinforcement, and repeated this procedure until the child began to perform the act in imitation of the trainer without assistance. Such procedures have not been applied to the understanding of instructions, such as "Bring me your shoes." It could be equally effective to have someone actually help the child perform such a request, provide immediate reinforcement, and continue until the retarded child could perform the requested act without assistance from another. This process may be far more effective than demonstrating what is expected, then waiting for imitation to occur.

Accurate syntax in verbal expression is slow to develop in retarded children. Techniques for modifying and increasing the use of correct syntax are somewhat rare in the literature. Braine (11) and Berko (9) have approached some techniques for developing complex verbal behavior. The application of such techniques to retarded children has not been reported. Braine (11) demonstrated that children can make positional generalizations for words, but this occurred only after they had learned several appropriate responses in the simple artificial language being learned. Perhaps the retarded child should learn numerous correct syntactical structures by imitation before being expected to generalize them to new situations. This might be done through "expansion imitation" by the adult. If the retarded child uses such responses as "more," the expanded imitation by the speech pathologist might be "I want some more." When the child repeats the adult pattern, immediate reinforcement should follow. The effectiveness of such procedures cannot be reported because their use with retarded children has been quite limited.

Audition

The relationship of audition to comprehension of language is a very close one. Certainly the comprehension of language is largely dependent upon the adequacy of audition—not just the auditory acuity but also the central processing of meaningful sound combinations. Eisenson (19) has speculated that individuals who have difficulty learning language may require longer "interval times" to receive successive sound elements. Mentally retarded children require longer times to accomplish many acts, both physical and mental. It is likely that they may require longer time intervals to receive and process the sound elements of language. In addition to providing signals of adequate loudness, it may be important to vary the rate of sound presentation. Little work has been done in this area and little can be suggested in the way of possible therapy techniques.

Liberman (57) has proposed a motor perception theory of speech that holds implications for training audition abilities. He contends that it is difficult to recognize sounds that one cannot produce. If the retarded child cannot produce sequences of sounds, is it possible that he cannot perceive sequences of sounds? These and many other questions must be answered before extensive specific language therapy techniques can be described with assurance of their effectiveness. In the meantime, the clinician may find that adapting some of the techniques used in teaching language to the deaf and the aphasic will be useful.

General procedures

A general theory of language and speech modification is not well developed at this time. Several approaches have been mentioned as they relate to specific problems. Some discussion of specific types of therapy might be useful to those speech pathologists and audiologists who are working with retarded children. These suggestions are offered as reminders that some of the traditional approaches have value with the retarded when applied on a selective basis, and that the more recent techniques should be used and evaluated.

The communication-centered approach described by Backus and Beasley (5) offers many opportunities to develop and practice patterns of speech and language that are useful to the retarded individual. These sessions, when kept simple, provide much realism and much reward for correct responses. The method provides the degree of flexibility that allows the speech pathologist to plan responses that are appropriate for the individuals and are within their capability.

Several references were made to the use of strong auditory stimulation as a means of providing a pattern for the retarded child to imitate. Milisen (71) has discussed the value of this method with nonretarded children, and provided careful descriptions of the procedure. It is important to remember that the sensory intake avenues of hearing and vision may not be so efficient in the retarded child. Therefore, the use of all avenues to provide stimulation to the retarded child is essential.

It seems simple enough to talk about using imitation as a procedure for modifying language patterns and articulation errors. It becomes more complicated when one remembers that some retarded children do not imitate. Mowrer (72) has provided one of the most comprehensive discussions of this process of imitation. The description might be useful to the speech pathologist faced with the need to establish imitation in language activities. In addition, Fay's (20) work on echolalia should prove helpful.

Behavior modification based on operant conditioning principles has been mentioned several times as a useful procedure for changing speech and language behavior of the retarded child. The technique has been used rather extensively in some centers, and is believed to be quite promising. Spradlin *et al.* (84) have provided the most comprehensive description of the use of this technique with retardates; it would be well for the clinician to study this work thoroughly.

At the University of Oregon Medical School's Mental Retardation Center, the operant conditioning approach also has been used with considerable success. In this setting behavior modification therapy is carried on principally by three professionals: a clinical psychologist, a social worker, and a speech pathologist. Working as a team, these three individuals systematically observe and record the verbal behavior of the child in relation to his family at home and in clinic situations. After a comprehensive description of this verbal behavior is available, a treatment plan is devised, which involves the mother and sometimes other members of the family.

Stated simply, the mother-child relationship is modified in the laboratory situation, where changes in behavior on the part of both are brought about by application of the principles of reinforcement and reward. This procedure is not new to speech pathology, but it does bring about a more systematic organization of observed behavior and applied principles of reinforcement for improvement.

It should be pointed out that mother is not always involved in the treatment process. The same principles are applied in a clinician-child relationship or a child-child relationship, or in any other situations in which there may be opportunity for improvement of language behavior. While this technique is not a panacea to be applied indiscriminately, it certainly bears study by the alert clinician; at this writing, the method offers a great deal of promise—especially if it is approached with a creative, unbiased attitude and a willingness to expand and experiment beyond the basic principles.

Summary

This chapter may be disappointing to some speech pathologists or audiologists who hoped to find a great many specific techniques to apply in therapy sessions. However, to individuals who are seeking ways of dealing effectively with the speech, language, and hearing problems of the retarded individual, it will be reassuring to learn that some of the traditional methods have value and that new methods can and should be developed.

The effectiveness of training retarded individuals to improve their communication skills is dependent in large measure on selecting the procedure that will directly modify the observed deficiency. This does not differ in any major way from the effectiveness of speech, language, and hearing therapy with nonretarded individuals. In all areas of language training, there is a constant search for more effective procedures. Hopefully, this search will continue as long as professional help is available to the language-handicapped individuals.

A study of references at the end of this chapter may suggest additional approaches to language training of retardates. The suggested ways of relating methods currently available to the basic processes involved in adequate communication may serve as a stimulus to the speech pathologist and audiologist to explore techniques and methods not currently described in books.

Supplemental references

Arnold, Ruth Gifford. "Speech Rehabilitation for the Mentally Handicapped." *Exceptional Children,* Vol. 22, No. 2, 1955. Pp. 50–52 and 76–83.

Barker, Janet, and G. England. "A Numerical Measure of Articulation: Further Developments." *Journal of Speech and Hearing Disorders,* Vol. 27, No. 1, 1962. Pp. 23–27.

Board of Education of the City of New York. *Speech for the Retarded Child.* New York, Publications Sales Office, 1960. P. 98.

Cabanas, R. "Some Findings in Speech and Voice Therapy Among Mentally Deficient Children." *Folia Phoniatrica,* Vol. 6, No. 1, 1954. Pp. 34–37.

Cooper, S. "Speech Therapy for the Mentally Retarded." *Journal of Rehabilitation in Asia,* Vol. 5, 1964. Pp. 48–49.

Kastein, S. "An Analysis of the Development of Language in Children with Special Reference to Dysacusis." In Hellmuth, J., ed., *The Special Child in Century 21.* Seattle, Wash., Special Child Publications of Seguin School, 1964.

Magliato, R. "How We Can Meet the Speech Needs of the Adolescent Retardate." *Digest of the Mentally Retarded,* Vol. 1, 1964. Pp. 121–125.

Massengill, R., Jr., G. Quinn, K. L. Pickrell, and Carole Levenson. "Therapeutic Exercise and Velopharyngeal Gap." *The Cleft Palate Journal,* Vol. 5, January, 1968. Pp. 44–47.

Mecham, M. J. "The Development and Application of Procedures for Measuring Speech Improvement in Mentally Defective Children." *American Journal of Mental Deficiency,* Vol. 60, No. 2, 1955. Pp. 301–306.

Renfrew, Catherine E. "Speech Problems of Backward Children." *Speech Pathology and Therapy,* Vol. 2, No. 1, 1959. Pp. 34–38.

Salzinger, Suzanne, K. Salzinger, Stephanie Portnay, Judith Eckman, Pauline M. Bacon, M. Deutsch, and J. Zubin. "Operant Conditioning of Continuous Speech in Young Children." *Child Development,* Vol. 33, No. 3, 1962. Pp. 683–695.

Webb, C. E., and S. Kinde. "Speech, Language, and Hearing of the Mentally Retarded." In Baumeister, A. N., ed. *Mental Retardation.* Chicago, Aldine Publishing Company, 1967.

Wilson, F. B. "Efficacy of Speech Therapy with Educable Mentally Retarded Children." *Journal of Speech and Hearing Disorders,* Vol. 9, No. 3, 1966. Pp. 423–433.

CHAPTER *9*

Summary and notes on trends for the future

The foregoing chapters have attempted to review many of the traditional concepts of mental retardation as well as to present some of the newer concepts that involve a broader way of thinking about and functioning toward the mentally retarded. We have pointed out that over the years, and especially in recent years, attitudes toward the mentally retarded and approaches toward their management have undergone a great deal of change. The most significant aspect of this change is that there currently is a widespread interest among a great many professionals and lay persons in problems of the retardate, who is no longer a "forgotten child." Instead, many of the resources of an entire nation are being marshaled toward

173

finding methods of prevention, recognition, management, education, and employment of the retarded. The justification for this attitude becomes obvious when we realize that there are approximately six-million retarded persons in this country, and most of them are children. When we realize that mental retardation disables many more persons than any other handicap, and almost as many as all other handicaps combined, such widespread interest becomes of great significance. The wonder of it is that recognition and action were so long in coming.

We have pointed out that another new concept of mental retardation is that it is a multiple handicap rather than a single entity circumscribed by an intelligence quotient. We have described the multiplicity of intellectual, physical, behavioral, and cultural aspects of the mentally retarded population. No longer can we accept the diagnosis of mental retardation based on an isolated intelligence test followed by a rigid classification of mental subnormality while the medical, social, and educational needs of the child are largely ignored.

The study, preventive aspects, diagnosis, and management of retardates today require the combined skills of many professionals in medicine, dentistry, education, psychology, social work, nursing, physical and occupational therapy, speech pathology and audiology, the home, and the community. This being the case, the speech pathologist or audiologist concerned with the mentally retarded must understand not only the multiplicity of the problems but also the multiplicity of ways to deal with the problems. He no longer can afford *not* to be a part of the diagnostic process if he is to have any function in the treatment. Beyond this, he cannot afford to approach treatment in isolation, but must do so in terms of the totality of the problems and the other individuals, the home, and the community involved, as well as the prognostic potentialities in the situation.

Such being the case, the communication specialist, then, also must be a "multihandicap, multidiscipline specialist" if he is to work successfully with the retarded. He must be willing to work as a team member in whatever role is needed for a particular situation. Further than that, he should become a strong leader in developing the multidiscipline approach to the retarded child and in the molding of the many individuals and units necessary to comprise a team required for handling the retarded.

Because mental retardation is a multifaceted condition, the communication problems of the mentally retarded also are many and varied. It has been shown that the speech and language problems of the retarded are not simply problems of delay related to the amount of mental retardation. The retarded child is subject to all of the influences that may cause deviations in the development of communication skills in any child. In addition to this, the delay factors relate not only to the amount of mental retardation but also to many other factors peculiar to multiply handicapped individuals. For these reasons, diagnosis of communication problems in retardates requires extensive differential procedures. This calls for very sophisticated knowledge and skills on the part of the communication specialist. He needs not only to know a great deal about communication disorders in all their forms but also must have a solid, basic understanding of normal communication development and what is involved in language learning by the nonhandicapped child.

In addition to understanding extensive differential diagnosis, the communication specialist will need to approach therapy from many directions. He will find an enormous challenge for creativity, flexibility, and the skill to use any of the many resources at hand beyond his own familiar procedures. In particular, the communication clinician will need to possess the skill and willingness to put many of the tasks of developing the communication skills of the retarded in the hands of others who are working with him—such as the physical or occupational therapist, the psychologist, the social worker, the parents, and the classroom teachers. Finally, he will need considerable sensitivity and judgment in setting and adhering to realistic and attainable goals.

The future

It has been shown that attitudes and approaches toward mental retardation have undergone a great change in recent years. One of the most significant results of this change is to be seen in the participation of the federal government in the establishment of programs for research, diagnosis, treatment, and prevention of conditions causing mental retardation, as well as in the education and training of the retarded and education and training of professionals to work with them. This participation has been nationwide and has resulted in massive efforts in many localities for the establishment of truly comprehensive programs to deal with retardates.

One of these programs is of paramount interest to the speech pathologist and audiologist concerned with mental retardation, and also to the entire profession of speech pathology and audiology. This is the establishment of "university-affiliated" mental retardation centers throughout the country. There are a number of such centers in many parts of the United States, and more to be established. These centers are supported by a cooperative arrangement between the Department of Health, Education and Welfare and the states involved. They are established on the assumption that the combined resources of university programs affiliated with medical schools or other medical facilities can offer the best services to meet the future needs of retarded individuals. These centers are established principally on university and medical school campuses, with support of both federal and state funds for the building of comprehensive research, diagnostic, treatment, and educational facilities and programs.

The philosophy underlying the establishment of these centers, expressed by many persons in the federal agencies involved, is a tremendously significant one for the speech pathologist and audiologist. No longer do these persons regard retardates in the traditional narrow sense. They have accepted the fact that the mentally retarded child is a multiply handicapped child. They have gone even further in accepting the interpretation that, regardless of a child's IQ score, he may be considered retarded if he has a disability sufficient to keep him from reaching his potential educational, physical, or social development. For example, the child with a severe learning disorder but who might show normal intelligence may be considered to be a "retarded" child.

In a like manner, the child who comes from a severely deprived environment may be retarded in many aspects of development—physical, mental, social, and in communication skills. Even though he may have the mental potential for adequate functioning, he is nonetheless "retarded" until this potential can be developed. More important, the child with a communication disorder, yet with normal intelligence, also may come under the same classification if his communication disorder causes such disability that he cannot function adequately as a social being.

This broad concept of retardation should have a profound effect on the future of the speech and hearing profession and the functioning of many individuals in it. Perhaps the majority of children and adults seen in speech and hearing clinics for major communication disabilities would come under a classification of "retardation" when the word is used in this broad sense. Actually, this philosophy is in agreement with that of many speech pathologists and audiologists who have felt that a large number of children seen in speech and hearing clinics and school programs present a picture of retardation and, in fact, actually are mentally retarded according to traditional standards. In any event, it may be that most of the severe speech and hearing problems may in one way or another, or at some time or another, come within the province of the university-affiliated mental retardation center.

The great opportunity this opens for speech pathologists and audiologists is that all of the medical and allied resources needed for adequate diagnosis and treatment will be at hand. In addition, there will be adequate facilities and the opportunity to train students in this broad concept of rehabilitation of the child with speech and hearing handicaps, as well as to teach courses in these areas. Finally, the tremendous potential for research in such centers is perhaps the most exciting aspect of all. Here will be readily available populations of children and adults with all kinds of communication disorders, and the facilities will be adequate to conduct research related to all of them.

In addition, such centers will provide for learning more about speech and language development in children, the specific nature of communication disorders, the methods for modifying communicative behavior, and educational possibilities. In one sense, the investigator will have most of the aspects connected with speech and language development available for "slow-motion" study in children. The same will be true of communication disorders. Retardates are chronologically older and, therefore, sometimes make better research subjects. Yet their speech and language functions can be and often are similar to those of younger children, and develop over a longer period of time. Frequently the very early stages of speech and language growth can be studied in an older, relatively more social being who should be more amenable to research procedures.

The university-affiliated centers may be the most dramatic recent development in the field of retardation, but there are other significant events as well. The President's Committee on Mental Retardation, referred to earlier, makes continuous study of the problems of mental retardation in the United States and reports yearly, with recommendations for further government action. Many states have established rather wide-range programs for the mentally retarded through child development clinics, mental health clinics, public health departments, and by paying increasing attention to the mentally retarded through the school systems. Many of these programs and state institutions for the mentally retarded are seeking help from speech pathologists and audiologists for the diagnosis and treatment of communication disorders.

Medicare and Medicaid programs are creating an increasing demand for speech and hearing services for many kinds of handicapped individuals, including the mentally retarded. Finally, speech and hearing clinics in an increasing number are paying closer attention to this population and to the disorders presented by retardates. Such developments as these make it obvious that the speech pathologist and the audiologist must have considerable information and skill, as well as interest, in studying and working with individuals who have hearing, speech, and language problems related to mental retardation.

Bibliography

1. Ammons, R. B., and Helen S. Ammons. *The Full-Range Picture Vocabulary Test*. Missoula, Mont., Psychological Test Specialists, 1948.
2. Anderson, D. "Mental Retardation and Hearing Impairment." Unpublished paper. Oregon State Board of Health, Portland, Ore., 1964.
3. Anderson, Ruth M., Madeline Miles, and Patricia A. Matheny. *Language Development Scale*. Children's Hospital, Denver, Colo., 1963.
4. *A Study of Child Services in the Portland, Oregon, Public Schools*. Mimeographed publication of the Department of Research and Measurements. Portland, Ore., 1963. Pp. 275–288.
5. Backus, Ollie, and Jane Beasley. *Speech Therapy with Children*. Boston, Houghton Mifflin, 1951.
6. Baer, D. M., R. S. Peterson, and J. A. Sherman. "Building an Imitative Repertoire by Programming Similarity Between Child

181

and Model as Discriminative for Reinforcement." Paper read at the Biennial Meeting of the Society for Research in Child Development, Minneapolis, Minn., 1965.

7. Bangs, Tina E. "Evaluating Children with Language Delay." *Journal of Speech and Hearing Disorders,* Vol. 26, No. 1, 1961. Pp. 6–18.

8. Barker, Janet O., and G. England. "A Numerical Measure of Articulation: Further Developments." *Journal of Speech and Hearing Disorders,* Vol. 27, No. 1, 1962. Pp. 23–27.

9. Berko, Jean. "The Child's Learning of English Morphology." *Word,* Vol. 14, No. 2, 1958. Pp. 150–177.

10. Black, J. W. "The Pressure Component in the Production of Consonants." *Journal of Speech and Hearing Disorders.* Vol. 15, No. 3, 1950. Pp. 207–210.

11. Braine, M. D. S. "The Ontogeny of English Phrase Structure: The First Phrase." *Language,* Vol. 39, No. 1, 1963. Pp. 1–13.

12. Cardwell, Viola E. *Cerebral Palsy Advances in Understanding and Care.* New York, Association for the Aid of Crippled Children, 1956. Pp. 341–346.

13. Carson, Wilma, ed. "A Medical-Dental Approach to Evaluate Mentally Retarded Children." Unpublished paper, University of Oregon Medical School, Portland, Ore., 1965.

14. Crabtree, Margaret. *The Houston Test for Language Development.* Mimeographed publication, Houston, Tex., University of Houston.

15. Critchley, E. *Speech Origins and Development.* Springfield, Ill., Charles C Thomas, 1967.

16. Darley, F. L. *Diagnosis and Appraisal of Communication Disorders.* Englewood Cliffs, N.J., Prentice-Hall Foundations of Speech Pathology Series, 1964. Pp. 41–51.

17. Döring, G. K. "Ursachen und Vermeidung der Frühgeburt." In Ewerbeck, H. and L. Friedberg, eds. *Die Ubërgangstorungen des Neugeborenen und die Bekämpfung der perinatalen Mortalitat (Symposium).* Stuttgart, Germany. Georg Thieme, 1965. Pp. 137–140. English abstract in *Mental Retardation Abstracts,* Vol. 4, No. 2, U. S. Department of Health, Education and Welfare, 1967. P. 195.

18. Dunn, L. M. *Peabody Picture Vocabulary Test.* Nashville, Tenn., American Guidance Service, 1959.

19. Eisenson, J. "Developmental Aphasia: A Speculative View with Therapeutic Implications." *Journal of Speech and Hearing Disorders,* Vol. 33, No. 1, 1968. Pp. 3–13.
20. Fay, W. H. "Childhood Echolalia." *Folia Phoniatrica,* Vol. 19, No. 4, 1967. Pp. 297–306.
21. Fletcher, S. G., R. L. Casteel, and Doris P. Bradley. "Tongue Thrust Swallow, Speech Articulation, and Age." *Journal of Speech and Hearing Disorders,* Vol. 26, No. 3, 1961. Pp. 201–208.
22. Freeman, G. G., and Jean Lukens. "A Speech and Language Program for Educable Mentally Handicapped Children." *Journal of Speech and Hearing Disorders,* Vol. 27, No. 3, 1962. Pp. 285–287.
23. French, N. R., C. W. Carter, and W. Koenig. "The Words and Sounds of Telephone Conversation." *Bell System Technical Journal,* Vol. 9, 1930. Pp. 290–324.
24. Fries, C. C. *The Structure of English.* New York, Harcourt, Brace, & World, 1952.
25. Gardner, J. W. *President's Committee on Mental Retardation, A First Report.* Washington, D.C., U. S. Government Printing Office, 0-269-237, 1967. Pp. 1–32.
26. Gershenson, S., and M. Schreiber. "Mentally Retarded Teenagers in a Social Group." *Children,* Vol. 10, No. 3, 1963. Pp. 104–109.
27. Gesell, A., and Katherine S. Amatruda. *Developmental Diagnosis: Normal and Abnormal Child Development,* 2nd ed. New York, Paul B. Hoeber, 1947.
28. Goddard, Lynnette. "A Normative Study of Oral Breath Pressure in Children." Unpublished M.A. Thesis, Iowa City, Iowa, University of Iowa, 1959.
29. Gray, G. W., and C. M. Wise. *The Bases of Speech,* 3rd ed., New York, Harper & Row, 1959.
30. Greenbaum, M., and J. A. Buehler. "Further Findings on the Intelligence of Children with Cerebral Palsy." *Journal of Mental Deficiency,* Vol. 28, No. 2, 1960. Pp. 261–264.
31. Gullickson, J. "Dental Diagnosis and Treatment of Mentally Retarded Children." Unpublished paper, University of Oregon Medical School, Portland, Ore., 1966.
32. Harrison, S. "Integration of Developmental Language Activities

with an Educational Program for Mentally Retarded Children."
American Journal of Mental Deficiency, Vol. 63, May, 1959.
Pp. 967–970.

33. Heber, R. "A Manual on Terminology and Classification in
Mental Retardation." Monograph Supplement, 2nd ed., *American Journal of Mental Deficiency,* Vol. 65, No. 1, 1960–61.
Pp. 499–500.

34. Hellmuth, J., ed. *The Special Child in Century 21.* Special
Child Publications of the Seguin School, Seattle, Wash., 1964.

35. Hollis, J. H., and C. E. Gorton. "Training Severely and Profoundly Developmentally Retarded Children." *Mental Retardation,* Vol. 5, No. 4, 1967. Pp. 20–24.

36. Hollien, H., and R. H. Copeland. "Speaking Fundamental
Frequency (SFF) of Mongoloid Girls." *Journal of Speech and
Hearing Disorders,* Vol. 30, No. 4, 1965. Pp. 344–349.

37. Holmes, R. W., and L. P. Pelletier, Jr. *The Pineland Hospital
Speech and Hearing Survey, 1964–1966: Part Two.* Pownal,
Maine, Pineland Hospital and Training Center, 1966. Pp. 1–27.

38. Horstman, D. M. "Rubella and the Rubella Syndrome: New
Epidemiologic and Virologic Observations." *California Medicine,* Vol. 102, June, 1965. Pp. 397–403.

39. Huxley, J. E., H. O. Mayer, and A. Hoffer. "Schizophrenia as a
Genetic Morphism." *Nature,* Vol. 204, October, 1964. Pp. 220–221.

40. Ingram, Christine P. *Education of the Slow Learning Child,* 3rd
ed., New York, Ronald Press, 1960.

41. Irwin, Ruth B. "Oral Language for Slow Learning Children."
American Journal of Mental Deficiency, Vol. 64, No. 1, 1959.
Pp. 32–40.

42. Jervis, G. A. "Medical Aspects of Mental Retardation." *Journal
of Rehabilitation,* Vol. 28, No. 6, 1962. Pp. 34–36.

43. Johnson, W., F. L. Darley, and D. C. Spriestersbach. *Diagnostic
Methods in Speech Pathology.* New York, Harper & Row, 1962.

44. Joint Expert Committee. *The Mentally Subnormal Child,
Technical Report.* World Health Organization, 1955.

45. Jordan, T. E. *The Mentally Retarded.* Columbus, Ohio, Charles
E. Merrill Books, 1961. Pp. 2–3, p. 100, p. 235.

46. Kanner, L. *Child Psychiatry,* 3rd ed., Springfield, Ill., Charles
C Thomas, 1957.

47. Kempthorne, E. *The Design and Analysis of Experiments.* New York, John Wiley, 1952. Pp. 1–9.
48. Kendall, D. "Developmental Aspects of Audition." Unpublished paper presented at Symposium on Language Development and Language Disorders, Portland, Ore., May, 1965.
49. Kennedy, J. F. "A Statement by the President." *Journal of Rehabilitation,* Vol. 28, No. 6, 1962. Pp. 22–23.
50. Kirk, S. A., and J. J. McCarthy. *Illinois Test of Psycholinguistic Abilities: Examiner's Manual.* Urbana, Ill., University of Illinois Institute for Research on Exceptional Children, 1961.
51. Kirk, S. A., M. B. Karnes, and W. D. Kirk. *You and Your Retarded Child: A Manual for Parents.* New York, Macmillan Company, 1955.
52. Kodman, F., Jr. "The Incidence of Hearing Loss in Mentally Retarded Children." *American Journal of Mental Deficiency,* Vol. 62, No. 1, January, 1958. Pp. 675–678.
53. Lassers, L., and G. Low. *A Study of the Relative Effectiveness of Different Approaches of Speech Training for Mentally Retarded Children.* San Francisco State College and U. S. Office of Education, 1960.
54. Leberfeld, Doris T. "Speech Therapy." In *The Evaluation and Treatment of the Mentally Retarded Child in Clinics,* National Association for Retarded Children, Inc., New York, 1956. P. 67.
55. Lerea, L. "Assessing Language Development." *Journal of Speech and Hearing Research,* Vol. 1, No. 1, 1958. Pp. 75–85.
56. Levenson, A., and J. A. Bigler. *Mental Retardation in Infants and Children.* Chicago, Year Book Publishers, 1960.
57. Liberman, P. *Intonation, Perception, and Language.* Cambridge, Massachusetts, Research Monograph No. 30, The M.I.T. Press, 1967. Pp. 162–171.
58. Lillywhite, H. S. "Developmental Aspects of Mentally Retarded Children." Unpublished paper, University of Oregon Medical School, Portland, Ore., 1958.
59. Lloyd, L. L., and R. D. Frisina. *The Audiologic Assessment of the Mentally Retarded, Proceedings of a National Conference.* Parsons, Kans., Parsons State Hospital and Training Center, 1965. P. 265.
60. Lloyd, L. L., and J. J. Reid. "The Incidence of Hearing Impairment in an Institutionalized Mentally Retarded Popula-

tion." *American Journal of Mental Deficiency,* Vol. 71, No. 4, 1967. Pp. 746–763.

61. Lovaas, O. I., J. P. Perloff, B. F. Perloff, and B. Schaeffer. "Acquisition of Imitative Speech by Schizophrenic Children." *Science,* Vol. 151, No. 3711. Pp. 705–707.

62. *Manual for Evaluation of Speech, Hearing and Language.* Crippled Children's Division, University of Oregon Medical School, Portland, Ore., 1958.

63. McCarthy, Dorothea. "The Language Development of the Preschool Child." *Child Welfare Monographs,* No. 4, Minneapolis, Minn., University of Minnesota Press, 1930.

64. Marge, M. "Committee on Language Development and Disorders." *ASHA,* Vol. 9, No. 10, 1967. P. 415.

65. Marshall, Nancy. "Oral Deviations and Speech and Language Disorders in 200 Mentally Retarded Children." Unpublished paper, University of Oregon Medical School, Portland, Ore., 1967. P. 5.

66. Masland, R. L., S. B. Sarason, and T. Gladwin. *Mental Subnormality.* New York, Basic Books, 1958. P. 2.

67. Matthews, J. "Speech Problems of the Mentally Retarded." In Travis, L. E., ed. *Handbook of Speech Pathology.* New York, Appleton-Century-Crofts, 1957. Pp. 531–551.

68. Mecham, M. J. *Verbal Language Development Scale.* Nashville, Tenn., Educational Test Bureau, Educational Publishers, 1959.

69. Michal-Smith, H., and S. Kastein. *The Special Child, Diagnosis, Treatment, Habilitation.* Seattle, Wash., New School for the Special Child, Bureau of Publications, 1962. P. 13.

70. Michel, J. F., and J. R. Carney. "Pitch Characteristics of Mongoloid Boys." *Journal of Speech and Hearing Disorders,* Vol. 29, No. 2, May, 1964. Pp. 121–125.

71. Milisen, R., ed. "The Disorder of Articulation: A Systematic Clinical and Experimental Approach," *Journal of Speech and Hearing Disorders,* Monograph Supplement 4, 1954. Pp. 1–16.

72. Mowrer, O. H. *Learning Theory and the Symbolic Processes.* New York, John Wiley, 1960.

73. Penfield, W., and L. Roberts. *Speech and Brain Mechanisms.* Princeton, N.J., Princeton University Press, 1959. P. 257.

74. Powers, Margaret H. "Functional Disorders of Articulation—Symptomatology and Etiology." In Travis, L. E., ed., *Hand-*

book of Speech Pathology. New York, Appleton-Century-Crofts, 1957. Pp. 707–768.

75. Rheingold, Harriet L. "The Development of Social Behavior in the Human Infant." *Child Development Monographs,* Serial 107, Vol. 31, No. 5, 1966. Pp. 1–16.

76. Robinson, H. B., and Nancy M. Robinson. *The Mentally Retarded Child: A Psychological Approach.* New York, McGraw-Hill, 1965. Pp. 372–373.

77. Ryan, M. D., and Joyce H. Stewart. "The Use of Textured Pictures as Reinforcement in Meaningful Sound Identification Audiometry." In Lloyd, L. L., and D. R. Frisina, eds. *The Audiologic Assessment of the Retarded: Proceedings of a National Conference.* Parsons, Kans., Parsons State Hospital and Training Center, 1965.

78. Schiefelbusch, R. L., and H. V. Bair. "Language Studies of Mentally Retarded Children." *Journal of Speech and Hearing Disorders,* Monograph Supplement Number 10, January, 1963. P. 107.

79. Schlanger, B. B. "Speech Therapy with Mentally Retarded Children." *Journal of Speech and Hearing Disorders,* Vol. 23, No. 3, 1958. Pp. 298–301.

80. Schlanger, B. B., and R. H. Gottsleben. "Analysis of Speech Defects Among the Institutionalized Mentally Retarded." *Journal of Speech and Hearing Disorders,* Vol. 22, No. 1, 1957. Pp. 98–103.

81. Shelton, R. L., and J. F. Bosma. "Maintenance of the Pharyngeal Airway." *Journal of Applied Physiology,* Vol. 17, No. 2, 1962. Pp. 209–214.

82. Skinner, B. F. *Verbal Behavior.* New York, Appleton-Century-Crofts, 1957.

83. Smith, Madorah E. "An Investigation of the Development of the Sentence and the Extent of Vocabulary in Young Children." Iowa City, Iowa, *University of Iowa Studies in Child Welfare,* Vol. 3, No. 5, 1935.

84. Spradlin, J. E. "Procedures for Evaluating Processes Associated with Receptive and Expressive Language." In Schiefelbusch, R. L., R. H. Copeland, and J. O. Smith, eds. *Language and Mental Retardation,* New York, Holt, Rinehart & Winston, 1967.

85. Spreen, Otfried. "Language Functions in Mental Retardation, A Review, II. Language in Higher Level Performance." *American Journal of Mental Deficiency,* Vol. 70, 1966. Pp. 351–362.
86. Telford, C. W., and J. M. Sawrey. *The Exceptional Individual.* Englewood Cliffs, N.J., Prentice-Hall, 1967.
87. Templin, Mildred C. *Certain Language Skills in Children: Their Development and Interrelationships.* Child Welfare Monographs, No. 26, Minneapolis, Minn., University of Minnesota Press, 1957.
88. Templin, Mildred, and F. L. Darley. *The Templin-Darley Tests of Articulation.* Iowa City, Iowa, University of Iowa Bureau of Education, Research, and Service, 1960.
89. Terman, L. M., and M. A. Merrill. *Stanford-Binet Intelligence Scale.* Boston, Houghton Mifflin, 1960.
90. Wechsler, D. *Wechsler Intelligence Scale for Children.* New York, Psychological Corporation, 1949.
91. Westlake, H., and D. Rutherford. *Speech Therapy for the Cerebral Palsied.* National Society for Crippled Children and Adults, Chicago, Illinois, 1961.
92. Wilson, D. K. "Children with Vocal Nodules." *Journal of Speech and Hearing Disorders,* Vol. 26, No. 1, 1961. Pp. 19–26.
93. Wortis, J. "Medical Treatment." In *The Evaluation and Treatment of the Mentally Retarded Child in Clinics.* New York, National Association for Retarded Children, 1956. Pp. 23–60.
94. Yannett, H. "Etiology and Pathology of Mental Retardation." In *The Evaluation and Treatment of the Mentally Retarded Child in Clinics.* New York, National Association for Retarded Children, 1956. Pp. 3–7.
95. Young, N. B. "Speech and Hearing Problems Among Mentally Retarded Children." Unpublished paper, University of Oregon Medical School, Portland, Ore., 1965.

Index

Index